One Breath at a Time Strategies for Stress Free Livin

By: Mustafa Nejem

CONTENTS

Part One:
Understanding Stress

The Nature of Stress:
What's Happening Inside Us

1. **Mindfulness and Awareness:**
   - **Mindfulness Meditation:**
   - Mindfulness contemplation includes paying consideration to the display minute without judgment. Standard hone can upgrade self-awareness and give a mental space to watch and react to stressors more successfully.
   - Begin with brief sessions and slowly increment the term as you gotten to be more comfortable. Center on your breath, substantial sensations, or a particular point of center to stay your consideration.
   - **Body Scan Meditation:**
   - This procedure includes efficiently bringing mindfulness to diverse parts of the body. It makes a difference in recognizing ranges of pressure and advancing unwinding.
   - Lie down or sit comfortably and bring consideration to each portion of your body, beginning from your toes and moving up to the best of your head. Take note any sensations, pressure, or unwinding, and permit any pressure to discharge as you center on each region.
   - **Mindful Walking:**
   - Join mindfulness into your day by day exercises, such as strolling. Pay consideration to the sensation of each step, the development of your body, and the environment around you.
   - Strolling mindfully can be a straightforward however capable way to break the cycle of push and bring your center back to the show minute.
   - **Breath Awareness Techniques:**
   - **Diaphragmatic Breathing:**
   - Put one hand on your chest and the other on your guts. Breathe in profoundly through your nose, permitting your stomach to extend. Breathe out gradually through pressed together lips, feeling your guts drop. This sort of breathing enacts the unwinding reaction, lessening push.
   - **Box Breathing:**
   - Breathe in for a tally of four, hold your breath for four checks, breathe out for four checks, and delay for another four checks some time recently rehashing. This strategy makes a difference control the breath and advances a sense of calm.

2. **Cognitive Restructuring:**
   - **Thought Records:**
   - Keep a thought diary to track and analyze negative contemplations. Record circumstances that trigger push, the related considerations, feelings, and the coming about behavior.
   - Recognize designs and topics to pick up knowledge into repeating negative thought designs. This self-awareness is pivotal for starting cognitive rebuilding.
   - **Cognitive Distancing:**
   - Step back and equitably assess your contemplations. Consider whether they are based on truths or suspicions.
   - Inquire yourself questions like, "Is there prove supporting this thought?" and "What would somebody else think almost this circumstance?" This makes a difference in picking up point of view and challenging unreasonable convictions.
   - **Mindfulness-Based Cognitive Therapy (MBCT):**
   - Combine mindfulness with cognitive rebuilding by joining mindfulness hones into the method.
   - Mindfulness makes a difference people watch their contemplations without quick judgment, permitting for a more objective examination and rebuilding of negative thought designs.
   - **Positive Affirmations:**
   - Make a list of positive confirmations that neutralize common negative convictions. Rehash these certifications routinely to strengthen a positive mentality.

- For illustration, on the off chance that the negative conviction is "I'm not great sufficient," supplant it with the certification, "I am competent and commendable of victory."
- **Gratitude Practice:**
- Develop a propensity of communicating appreciation day by day. This hone can move center absent from stressors by recognizing positive viewpoints of life.
- Type in down three things you're thankful for each day, cultivating a positive mentality and diminishing the affect of negative considerations.
- **Challenge Catastrophic Thinking:**
- Distinguish and challenge disastrous considering, where people envision the most noticeably awful conceivable results. Inquire yourself, "Is this the worst-case situation, or are there elective, more practical results?"

3. **Physical Activity:**
   - **Variety in Exercise:**
   - Investigate distinctive sorts of physical exercises to keep your schedule curiously and locks in. This may incorporate exercises like cycling, swimming, group sports, or quality preparing.
   - Blending up your work out schedule not as it were avoids boredom but moreover guarantees that diverse muscle bunches are locked in, advancing generally physical well-being.
   - **Outdoor Exercise:**
   - At whatever point conceivable, select open air exercises. Presentation to common daylight and new discuss can upgrade the mood-lifting benefits of work out.
   - Exercises like climbing, cycling, or indeed a basic walk within the park provide an opportunity to put through with nature and diminish push levels.
   - **Social Exercise:**
   - Combine physical movement with social interaction by taking an interest in gather classes or group sports. This cultivates a sense of community and gives a strong environment.
   - Having a workout buddy can too increment inspiration and make work out more pleasant.
   - **Mind-Body Exercises:**
   - Consolidate mind-body works out like yoga or tai chi into your schedule. These hones not as it were make strides physical wellness but too center on mindfulness and unwinding.
   - Mind-body works out can offer assistance lighten both physical and mental pressure, advancing a all encompassing approach to stretch administration.

4. **Healthy Lifestyle Habits:**
   - **Hydration:**
   - Remain satisfactorily hydrated by drinking sufficient water all through the day.
     Lack of hydration can contribute to sentiments of weariness and peevishness, affecting your capacity to manage with push.
   - Supplant sugary refreshments with water or home grown teas for a more beneficial hydration choice.
   - **Balanced Nutrition:**
   - Center on a well-rounded, adjusted slim down that incorporates a assortment of natural products, vegetables, entire grains, incline proteins, and sound fats.
   - Consolidate nutrient-dense nourishments wealthy in vitamins and minerals, such as verdant greens, berries, nuts, and greasy angle. These can emphatically affect your vitality levels and generally well-being.
   - **Mindful Eating:**
   - Hone careful eating by paying consideration to the flavors, surfaces, and sensations of each chomp. Dodge eating before screens or in a hurried way.
   - Careful eating advances a more beneficial relationship with nourishment and can offer assistance avoid stress-related gorging.

5. **Social Support:**
   - **Cultivate Meaningful Relationships:**
   - Focus on building deep and meaningful connections with friends, family, and community members.
   - Participate in activities that align with your interests, allowing you to connect with like-minded individuals and build a supportive social network.
   - **Regular Social Interactions:**

- Prioritize regular social interactions, whether in person, over the phone, or through virtual platforms. Consistent communication helps maintain strong connections and provides opportunities for mutual support.
- Schedule regular outings, gatherings, or virtual meet-ups to stay connected with loved ones.
- **Join Social Groups or Clubs:**
- Explore social groups, clubs, or organizations that align with your hobbies or interests. This can provide a built-in community and opportunities to meet new people who share similar passions.
- Engaging in group activities fosters a sense of camaraderie and expands your social support network.

6. **Time Management:**
   - **Prioritization Techniques:**
   - Use prioritization methods, such as the Eisenhower Matrix or the ABCD method, to categorize tasks based on urgency and importance.
   - Focus on high-priority tasks first, ensuring that essential and time-sensitive activities are addressed promptly.
   - **Time Blocking:**
   - Implement time blocking, where you allocate specific blocks of time to different tasks or categories of work. This helps create a structured schedule and minimizes the risk of multitasking.
   - Set aside dedicated time for focused work, breaks, and activities outside of work to maintain a healthy work-life balance.
   - **To-Do Lists:**
   - Create daily or weekly to-do lists to organize tasks and keep track of responsibilities. Break down larger projects into smaller, actionable steps.
   - Regularly update and review your to-do list to ensure it remains aligned with your priorities.

7. **Mind-Body Techniques:**
   - Explore practices like yoga, tai chi, or progressive muscle relaxation. These techniques combine physical movement with mindfulness, promoting relaxation and stress reduction.
   - Consider incorporating aromatherapy or soothing music into your routine. These sensory elements can have a calming effect on the nervous system.

Recognizing Stress Triggers in Your Daily Life

1. **Self-Reflection and Journaling:**
   - **Gratitude Journaling:**
   - In addition to recording stress triggers, incorporate gratitude journaling into your routine. At the end of each day, write down things you are grateful for.
   - Focusing on positive aspects of your life can counterbalance the impact of stressors and contribute to a more optimistic mindset.
   - **Emotion Wheel:**
   - Use an emotion wheel or chart to identify and label a wide range of emotions. This tool can help you pinpoint specific feelings associated with stress triggers.
   - Color-coding or highlighting emotions in your journal can visually represent the intensity and frequency of different emotions over time.
   - **Reflection Prompts:**
   - Incorporate reflection prompts into your journaling practice. For example, ask yourself questions like:
   - "What was the most challenging part of my day, and how did I handle it?"
   - "What activities or interactions brought me joy or relaxation today?"
   - **Stress Rating Scale:**
   - Develop a stress rating scale from 1 to 10 to quantify and track the intensity of stress experienced in various situations. This scale helps create a more objective measure of stress levels.
   - Analyze the entries over time to identify patterns in stress intensity and correlate them with specific triggers.
   - **Goal Setting and Progress Tracking:**
   - Set personal goals related to stress management and overall well-being. Document your progress regularly in your journal.
   - Reflect on the strategies and techniques you've implemented to address stress triggers and assess their effectiveness over time.
2. **Mindfulness and Body Awareness:**
   - **Breath Awareness Throughout the Day:**
   - Integrate breath awareness into your daily routine. Take moments throughout the day to focus on your breath, especially during transitions or moments of heightened stress.
   - Observing the rhythm of your breath fosters mindfulness, anchoring your attention in the present moment.
   - **Body Scan Meditation Variations:**
   - Experiment with different variations of body scan meditations. Some variations involve focusing on specific body parts sequentially, while others may emphasize observing sensations without a predetermined order.
   - Exploring various body scan techniques allows you to find the approach that resonates most with you.
   - **Sensory Grounding Techniques:**
   - Engage your senses as a way to anchor yourself in the present moment. Notice the sensations of touch, taste, sight, sound, and smell.
   - This sensory grounding can be particularly helpful during stressful situations, redirecting your focus away from stress triggers.
   - **Progressive Muscle Relaxation (PMR):**
   - Practice progressive muscle relaxation to release physical tension. Systematically tense and then release different muscle groups, starting from your toes and working your way up to your head.

- PMR is effective in promoting body awareness and reducing overall muscle tension associated with stress.

3. **Emotional Intelligence:**
   - **Emotion Journaling:**
   - Create an emotion journal to track and analyze your emotional experiences. Record the events or situations that trigger specific emotions and the associated thoughts and behaviors.
   - This ongoing record provides valuable insights into recurring emotional patterns and stress triggers.
   - **Mindful Observation of Emotions:**
   - Cultivate a mindful observation of your emotions as they arise. Instead of immediately reacting, take a moment to observe and acknowledge the emotion without judgment.
   - Mindful observation allows for a more measured and intentional response to stress triggers.
   - **Emotion Regulation Techniques:**
   - Learn and practice emotion regulation techniques to manage the intensity of emotions. Techniques such as deep breathing, progressive muscle relaxation, or visualization can help regulate emotional responses.
   - Integrate these techniques into your daily routine, especially during stressful situations.

4. **Stress Assessment Tools:**
   - Utilize stress assessment tools or questionnaires to evaluate your stress levels and identify common triggers. These tools often provide structured questions to pinpoint specific areas of concern.
   - Online resources or apps may offer stress assessments that provide personalized insights into your stressors.

5. **Environmental Cues:**
   - Pay attention to your physical environment and how it influences your stress levels. Clutter, noise, or lack of natural light can contribute to stress.
   - Create an environment conducive to relaxation and well-being, incorporating elements that promote calmness and comfort.

6. **Time-Tracking:**
   - Keep a detailed record of how you spend your time each day. Identify tasks or activities that consistently lead to stress.
   - Analyze whether time management strategies could alleviate stress related to specific responsibilities or deadlines.

7. **Social Interactions:**
   - **Relationship Inventory:**
   - Conduct a comprehensive inventory of your relationships. Evaluate the overall health and dynamics of your connections, considering both personal and professional spheres.
   - Identify relationships that bring positivity, support, and fulfillment, as well as those that may contribute to stress.
   - **Personal Values Alignment:**
   - Reflect on your core values and assess how well they align with your social interactions. Ensure that your relationships align with your values and contribute positively to your well-being.
   - This alignment fosters a sense of authenticity and reduces the likelihood of stress arising from conflicting values.
   - **Communication Styles Assessment:**
   - Reflect on communication styles within your social interactions. Assess whether open and effective communication is present or if there are challenges in understanding and being understood.
   - Identify opportunities for improving communication dynamics to prevent misunderstandings and reduce stress.

8. **Physical Health Assessment:**
   - Consider how your physical health may contribute to stress. Lack of sleep, poor nutrition, or inadequate exercise can amplify stress levels.
   - Regular health check-ups and assessments can help address underlying physical factors that may be contributing to stress.

9. **Workplace Stressors:**

- Assess your work environment for potential stressors. High workload, lack of control, unclear expectations, or poor relationships with colleagues can contribute to workplace stress.
- Communicate with supervisors about workload concerns and seek solutions to improve the work environment.

10. Behavioral Patterns:
- Identify recurring behavioral patterns during stressful situations. Do you tend to procrastinate, engage in negative self-talk, or resort to unhealthy coping mechanisms?
- Recognizing these patterns enables you to replace them with healthier responses and coping strategies.

11. Feedback from Others:
- **360-Degree Feedback:**
- Consider implementing a 360-degree feedback process, where feedback is gathered from multiple sources, including peers, supervisors, and direct reports.
- This comprehensive feedback approach provides a well-rounded view of your behavior and its impact on various aspects of your life.
- **Regular Check-Ins:**
- Establish regular check-ins with trusted friends, family, or colleagues to discuss overall well-being and stress levels. These check-ins provide a consistent forum for open communication.
- Frame discussions around mutual support and collaborative efforts to manage stress collectively.
- **Behavioral Observation Partnerships:**
- Form partnerships with individuals who are willing to observe and provide feedback on your behavior. This can be particularly effective in recognizing subtle changes that may indicate stress.
- Choose trustworthy individuals who can offer objective insights into your actions and demeanor.
- **Reflective Questioning:**
- Encourage others to ask reflective questions about your well-being and stress levels. Simple inquiries such as "How are you managing stress lately?" can open the door to meaningful conversations.
- Practice responding openly to such questions, fostering a culture of transparency.

12. Therapeutic Support:
- **Holistic Assessment with Therapist:**
- Engage in a comprehensive assessment with a mental health professional. Work collaboratively to explore various aspects of your life, including relationships, work, and personal history.
- A holistic assessment provides a thorough understanding of potential stressors and contributes to personalized treatment plans.
- **Psychoeducation on Stress:**
- Participate in psychoeducation sessions with your therapist to gain a deeper understanding of stress, its physiological effects, and common triggers.
- Educating yourself on stress empowers you to make informed decisions and implement effective coping strategies.
- **Mindfulness-Based Therapies:**
- Explore mindfulness-based therapies such as Mindfulness-Based Stress Reduction (MBSR) or Mindfulness-Based Cognitive Therapy (MBCT). These approaches integrate mindfulness practices with therapeutic interventions to enhance stress management.
- Mindfulness-based therapies promote present-moment awareness and cultivate a non-judgmental attitude toward stressors.

The Science of Stress:
How It Affects Your Body and Mind

1. **Mindfulness Meditation:**
   - **Mindful Walking:**
   - Integrate mindfulness into your daily routine by practicing mindful walking. Pay attention to each step, the sensation of your feet connecting with the ground, and the rhythm of your movement. This mindful approach to walking can be particularly grounding and stress-relieving.
   - **Body Awareness Meditation:**
   - Dedicate specific sessions to body awareness meditation. Focus on scanning your body from head to toe, observing sensations without judgment. This practice fosters a deeper connection between your mind and body, promoting relaxation and stress reduction.
   - **Loving-Kindness Meditation (Metta):**
   - Incorporate loving-kindness meditation into your mindfulness practice. Extend feelings of compassion and goodwill towards yourself and others.
     This practice not only reduces stress but also cultivates a positive and empathetic mindset.
   - **Mindful Eating:**
   - Transform your meals into opportunities for mindfulness. Pay attention to the colors, textures, and flavors of your food. Chew slowly and savor each bite, fully engaging your senses. Mindful eating fosters a healthier relationship with food and reduces stress associated with rushed meals.
2. **Biofeedback:**
   - Utilize biofeedback techniques to gain awareness and control over physiological responses to stress.
   - Employ biofeedback devices to monitor parameters such as heart rate or skin conductance. Through visualization and conscious control, learn to modulate these responses for stress reduction.
3. **Neurofeedback:**
   - Harness neurofeedback to train the brain to regulate stress-related neural patterns.
   - In a therapeutic setting, neurofeedback involves real-time monitoring of brainwave activity. Through feedback, individuals learn to shift brainwave patterns associated with stress.
4. **Heart Rate Variability (HRV) Training:**
   - **Heart Rate Variability (HRV) Biofeedback Apps:**
   - Use biofeedback apps that specifically target HRV training. These apps often provide real-time feedback on your HRV, guiding you through breathing exercises to optimize variability. They can be valuable tools for individuals looking to improve stress resilience.
   - **Coherence Training:**
   - Engage in coherence training, a specific form of HRV training that focuses on achieving physiological coherence. Coherence refers to a state where heart rate, breathing, and other physiological rhythms are synchronized. Biofeedback devices can assist in achieving and maintaining coherence, promoting a balanced nervous system.
   - **Morning Routine for HRV Enhancement:**
   - Incorporate HRV training into your morning routine. Begin the day with a few minutes of diaphragmatic breathing or guided rhythmic breathing exercises. This sets a positive tone for the day and establishes a foundation for improved stress resilience.
   - **Mindful HRV Breathing Breaks:**
   - Integrate short HRV breathing breaks throughout the day. Take a few minutes to focus on slow, deep breaths, paying attention to the natural rhythm of your breath. These micro-practices contribute to overall HRV improvement and stress reduction.
5. **Cognitive Restructuring:**
   - Identify and challenge negative thought patterns contributing to stress.

- Use cognitive restructuring to reframe negative self-talk. Replace irrational beliefs with positive affirmations, fostering a more balanced perspective.

6. **Gratitude Practices:**
   - **Gratitude Walks:**
   - Incorporate gratitude into your daily walks. As you walk, consciously reflect on the things you are grateful for—nature, health, relationships. This mindful approach transforms your walk into a gratitude practice, enhancing your mood and reducing stress.
   - **Express Gratitude Verbally:**
   - Express your gratitude verbally to others. Take time to thank people in your life, whether it's a friend, family member, or colleague.
     Verbalizing appreciation strengthens social connections and contributes to a positive, supportive environment.
   - **Gratitude Collages or Boards:**
   - Create visual representations of gratitude by making collages or boards. Collect images or words that symbolize aspects of your life you are thankful for. Displaying these visual reminders serves as a daily affirmation of gratitude.
   - **Gratitude in the Workplace:**
   - Integrate gratitude into the workplace. Recognize and appreciate the efforts of colleagues or team members. This practice fosters a positive work culture, reduces workplace stress, and enhances teamwork.
   - **Morning Gratitude Ritual:**
   - Establish a morning ritual dedicated to gratitude. Before starting your day, list three things you're grateful for. This sets a positive tone and helps shift your mindset towards appreciation, promoting resilience in the face of daily challenges.

7. **Progressive Muscle Relaxation (PMR):**
   - Release physical tension through systematic muscle relaxation.
   - Sequentially tense and then relax muscle groups, starting from toes to head. PMR promotes relaxation and alleviates the physical manifestations of stress.

8. **Yoga and Tai Chi:**
   - Incorporate mind-body practices like yoga and Tai Chi for holistic stress management.
   - Engage in gentle, flowing movements, combined with focused breathwork. These practices enhance physical flexibility, mental calmness, and stress resilience.

9. **Aromatherapy:**
   - **Aromatic Diffusers:**
   - Use aromatic diffusers to disperse essential oils throughout your living space. Experiment with scents like eucalyptus, peppermint, or citrus, each offering unique stress-relieving properties.
   - **Aromatherapy Massage:**
   - Incorporate aromatherapy into massages. Combine essential oils with carrier oils for a soothing massage experience. The combination of touch and scent promotes relaxation and alleviates muscular tension.
   - **Personalized Aromatherapy Blends:**
   - Create personalized aromatherapy blends.
     Experiment with combining different essential oils to create a scent that resonates with you. This tailored approach enhances the individualized benefits of aromatherapy.
   - **Aromatherapy Jewelry:**
   - Wear aromatherapy jewelry infused with essential oils. Diffuser necklaces or bracelets allow you to enjoy the calming scents throughout the day, providing a portable stress-relief solution.
   - **Aromatic Baths:**
   - Add a few drops of essential oils to your bathwater. Scents like lavender or chamomile can transform your bath into a calming and stress-relieving experience, promoting relaxation.

10. **Social Connection:**
    - Foster strong social connections as a buffer against stress.
    - Actively engage with friends, family, or community. Share experiences, concerns, and joys, creating a supportive network.

11. **Laughter Therapy:**
    - Incorporate humor to reduce stress and enhance mood.

- Watch comedies, attend laughter yoga sessions, or engage in activities that bring genuine laughter. Laughter releases endorphins, promoting a sense of well-being.

12. **Physical Activity:**
   - Engage in regular exercise to reduce stress hormones and boost mood.
   - Choose activities you enjoy, whether it's walking, jogging, cycling, or dancing. Consistent exercise contributes to overall well-being and stress management.

13. **Expressive Writing:**
   - Use expressive writing to process emotions and manage stress.
   - Set aside time to write about your thoughts and feelings regarding stressors. This practice enhances emotional clarity and may promote a sense of relief.

14. **Guided Imagery:**
   - Utilize guided imagery to create positive mental images and alleviate stress.
   - Close your eyes and imagine calming scenes or scenarios.
     Guided imagery can evoke relaxation responses, reducing stress levels.

15. **Art and Creativity:**
   - Express emotions through artistic pursuits for stress relief.
   - Engage in activities such as painting, drawing, or crafting. Creative expression provides an outlet for emotions and fosters a sense of accomplishment.

16. **Balanced Nutrition:**
   - Maintain a balanced and nutritious diet to support overall well-being.
   - Prioritize whole foods, including fruits, vegetables, and lean proteins. Adequate nutrition positively impacts the body's ability to cope with stress.

17. **Quality Sleep Hygiene:**
   - Prioritize sufficient and restful sleep for stress recovery.
   - Establish a consistent sleep routine, create a comfortable sleep environment, and limit screen time before bedtime. Quality sleep enhances emotional resilience.

18. **Breathwork Techniques:**
   - Leverage various breathwork techniques for immediate stress reduction.
   - Practice diaphragmatic breathing, box breathing, or alternate nostril breathing. Controlled breathing calms the nervous system and promotes relaxation.

19. **Setting Boundaries:**
   - Establish and communicate clear boundaries to prevent overwhelm.
   - Learn to say no when necessary, delegate tasks, and prioritize self-care. Setting boundaries helps manage stress by preventing overcommitment.

20. **Time Management:**
   - Organize tasks and set realistic goals to avoid feeling overwhelmed.
   - Break down larger tasks into smaller, manageable steps. Prioritize deadlines and be willing to delegate when possible to prevent undue stress.

Myths and Truths
About Stress

1. **Myth: Stress is always harmful.**
   - **Truth:** Not all stress is detrimental. There's a distinction between "eustress" (positive stress, such as excitement or challenge) and "distress" (negative stress). Eustress can be motivating and contribute to personal growth.
2. **Myth: Eliminating stress is the goal.**
   - **Myth: Stress is always harmful.**
   - **Truth:** While chronic and overwhelming stress can have negative effects, not all stress is harmful. Short-term stress, known as acute stress, can be a natural response to challenges and can even enhance performance. It's the prolonged exposure to high levels of stress that poses risks to health.
   - **Myth: Stress is solely a mental or emotional issue.**
   - **Truth:** Stress manifests in both psychological and physical ways. It can lead to various physical health issues such as headaches, digestive problems, and cardiovascular issues. Recognizing the interconnectedness of mental and physical well-being is crucial for comprehensive stress management.
   - **Myth: Stress is a sign of weakness.**
   - **Truth:** Experiencing stress is a common human experience and is not indicative of weakness. It's a natural response to challenges and can affect anyone. Acknowledging and addressing stress requires strength and resilience rather than being a reflection of personal inadequacy.
   - **Myth: Ignoring stress will make it go away.**
   - **Truth:** Ignoring stress doesn't make it disappear; in fact, it can exacerbate the situation. Addressing stress through proactive coping strategies, self-care, and seeking support is essential for long-term well-being. Ignoring stress can lead to more significant challenges down the line.
   - **Myth: Stress management is a one-size-fits-all approach.**
   - **Truth:** Effective stress management varies from person to person. Different techniques work for different individuals. It's essential to explore and identify personalized strategies that align with one's preferences, lifestyle, and specific stressors.
3. **Myth: Stress is solely a mental phenomenon.**
   - **Truth:** Stress affects both the mind and body.
     It involves physiological responses, such as the release of stress hormones and changes in heart rate. Recognizing these physical aspects is crucial for comprehensive stress management.
4. **Myth: Stress is always a sign of weakness.**
   - **Myth: Handling stress alone is a sign of strength.**
   - **Truth:** Seeking support and reaching out to others when facing stress is a strength, not a weakness. Collaborating with friends, family, or professionals fosters resilience and provides diverse perspectives and resources for effective stress management.
   - **Myth: Stress is a personal failure.**
   - **Truth:** Stress is not a reflection of personal failure. Life is filled with challenges, and stress is a natural response to these challenges. Understanding that everyone experiences stress allows individuals to approach it with self-compassion rather than self-blame.
   - **Myth: Admitting to stress is a vulnerability.**
   - **Truth:** Openly acknowledging and discussing stress is a courageous act. It promotes a culture of transparency, honesty, and shared experiences. By expressing vulnerability, individuals create opportunities for connection and support from those around them.
   - **Myth: Coping with stress independently is the ideal.**
   - **Truth:** While self-reliance is valuable, reaching out for help and collaborating with others is a powerful strategy for stress management. Social connections and support networks play a crucial role in providing emotional assistance during challenging times.

- **Myth: Stress is a sign of inadequate coping skills.**
- **Truth:** Stress is a common human experience, and its presence doesn't necessarily imply inadequate coping skills. Developing effective coping mechanisms is an ongoing process, and seeking to enhance these skills demonstrates a proactive approach to well-being.
- **Myth: High-achievers don't experience stress.**
- **Truth:** Even high-achieving individuals encounter stress. Success and ambition often come with increased responsibilities and pressures. Acknowledging stress and implementing healthy coping strategies are integral aspects of maintaining peak performance and well-being.
- **Myth: Expressing vulnerability during stress is a weakness.**
- **Truth:** Sharing vulnerability during times of stress builds trust and strengthens interpersonal relationships. Expressing emotions openly can create a supportive environment, allowing others to connect on a deeper level and offer assistance when needed.
- **Myth: Stress is a solitary experience.**
- **Truth:** Recognizing that stress is a shared human experience reduces feelings of isolation. Engaging in open conversations about stress fosters a sense of community and encourages the exchange of coping strategies and mutual support.
- **Myth: Suppressing emotions during stress shows strength.**
- **Truth:** Suppressing emotions can lead to increased stress and negative health outcomes. Acknowledging and expressing emotions in a healthy way is a strength. It allows for authentic self-expression and contributes to emotional well-being.
- **Myth: Asking for help is a sign of dependency.**
- **Truth:** Seeking help when stressed is a proactive and empowered choice. It reflects a willingness to collaborate and share burdens, leading to enhanced problem-solving and overall well-being.

5. **Myth: Time management eliminates stress.**
   - **Truth:** While effective time management is essential, it's not a cure-all for stress. Stress often stems from perception and emotional responses. Strategies like mindfulness, prioritization, and boundary-setting are equally crucial.
6. **Myth: Stress is only caused by external factors.**
   - **Truth:** Internal factors, such as perfectionism, negative self-talk, and unrealistic expectations, contribute significantly to stress. Recognizing and addressing these internal dynamics is vital for stress management.
7. **Myth: Ignoring stress is the best approach.**
   - **Truth:** Ignoring stress can lead to long-term negative consequences. It's essential to address stress through proactive strategies like self-care, seeking support, and developing coping mechanisms.
8. **Myth: Stress is always harmful to your health.**
   - **Truth:** Chronic, unmanaged stress can indeed have adverse health effects. However, acute stress responses, like the "fight or flight" reaction, are part of the body's natural survival mechanism. It's the chronic, prolonged stress that poses health risks.
9. **Myth: Alcohol and substance use alleviate stress.**
   - **Truth:** While substances may provide temporary relief, relying on them as coping mechanisms can lead to dependency and worsen stress in the long run. Healthy coping strategies, such as exercise or social support, are more sustainable.
10. **Myth: Stress affects everyone the same way.**
    - **Truth:** Individuals respond to stress differently based on factors like genetics, personality, and past experiences. Understanding one's unique stress response is crucial for tailoring effective stress management strategies.
11. **Myth: You can't control stress; it controls you.**
    - **Truth:** While certain stressors may be beyond control, individuals have agency over how they respond to stress. Developing coping skills, resilience, and adopting a positive mindset can empower individuals in managing stress.
12. **Myth: Stress is a purely psychological issue.**
    - **Truth:** Stress has physiological components, impacting various systems in the body Understanding the interconnectedness of mind and body is crucial for a holistic approach t stress management.

13. **Myth: Only major life events cause stress.**
    - **Truth:** Daily hassles and ongoing minor stressors can cumulatively impact well-being. Recognizing and addressing these smaller stressors is key to preventing them from escalating into more significant challenges.
14. **Myth: Stress management is a one-size-fits-all approach.**
    - **Truth:** Effective stress management is individualized. What works for one person may not work for another. It's essential to explore and tailor strategies that resonate with personal preferences and lifestyle.
15. **Myth: Stress is always visible.**
    - **Truth:** Some individuals may internalize stress, showing minimal outward signs. It's crucial to be attuned to both visible and subtle indicators of stress, such as changes in behavior, sleep patterns, or emotional well-being.
16. **Myth: Seeking help for stress is a sign of weakness.**
    - **Truth:** Seeking support for stress is a proactive and healthy step. Whether through friends, family, or professional resources, reaching out demonstrates self-awareness and a commitment to well-being.
17. **Myth: Once stress is managed, it's gone forever.**
    - **Truth:** Stress is an ongoing part of life. Managing stress is a dynamic process that requires continuous adaptation and learning. Building a repertoire of effective coping strategies is an ongoing journey.
18. **Myth: Stress management is time-consuming.**
    - **Truth:** Incorporating stress management into daily routines can be efficient. Short, consistent practices, such as mindfulness exercises or brief breaks, can have a significant impact on stress reduction without requiring extensive time commitments.
19. **Myth: Stress only affects adults.**
    - **Myth: Childhood is carefree, and children don't experience stress.**
    - **Truth:** Children encounter various stressors related to academic pressures, social dynamics, family challenges, and personal development. Acknowledging and addressing these stressors is vital for promoting a healthy and well-adjusted childhood.
    - **Myth: Children's stress is insignificant compared to adults.**
    - **Truth:** While children may face different stressors than adults, their experiences are significant and impactful.
    Children's stress can influence their emotional well-being, behavior, and overall development. Recognizing the importance of their stress is essential for providing appropriate support.
    - **Myth: Children are resilient, and stress doesn't affect them long-term.**
    - **Truth:** While children can be resilient, prolonged or unaddressed stress can have lasting effects on their mental health and well-being. Early interventions and supportive environments are crucial for minimizing the potential long-term impact of stress on children.
    - **Myth: Children's stress is always visible and easily identified.**
    - **Truth:** Children may not always express their stress overtly. Signs of stress in children can manifest as changes in behavior, sleep disturbances, academic challenges, or physical complaints.
20. **Myth: Stress is always negative.**
    - Truth: Stress can have positive aspects, such as motivating growth, creativity, and resilience. It's the balance between positive and negative stressors that contributes to overall well-being.

Part Two:
Laying the Foundations

The Power of Perception:
Viewing Stress Differently

1. **Mindfulness-Based Stress Reduction (MBSR):**
   - **Mindfulness Meditation:**
   - Mindfulness meditation involves focusing on the breath, sensations, or a specific point of focus to cultivate awareness of the present moment. Regular practice enhances the ability to observe thoughts and feelings without attachment or judgment, reducing the impact of stressors.
   - **Body Scan Meditation:**
   - A specific MBSR technique, the body scan meditation, involves systematically bringing attention to different parts of the body. This helps individuals become more attuned to physical sensations and promotes relaxation, easing the tension associated with stress.
   - **Walking Meditation:**
   - Incorporate walking meditation into daily routines. This involves mindful walking, paying attention to each step, the sensation of movement, and the surrounding environment. Walking meditation provides a dynamic way to practice mindfulness and reduce stress.
   - **Loving-Kindness Meditation (Metta):**
   - Extend mindfulness to the cultivation of positive emotions through loving-kindness meditation. Metta involves directing well-wishes and compassion towards oneself and others. This practice fosters a sense of connection and empathy, positively influencing the perception of stressors.
   - **Breath Awareness:**
   - Focus on breath awareness, a foundational aspect of mindfulness. By paying attention to the breath—its rhythm, depth, and sensation—individuals anchor themselves in the present moment. This simple yet powerful practice can be incorporated throughout the day for immediate stress relief.
2. **Cognitive Reframing:**
   - Practice cognitive reframing to shift negative perceptions of stress. Identify and challenge automatic negative thoughts associated with stressors, replacing them with more balanced and positive interpretations. This cognitive restructuring enhances resilience and reduces the emotional impact of stress.
3. **Stress Inoculation Training:**
   - Implement stress inoculation training, a cognitive-behavioral approach that involves gradually exposing oneself to stressors in a controlled manner. This process helps build resilience by allowing individuals to adapt to stressors incrementally, changing their perception of stress as overwhelming.
4. **Positive Psychology Interventions:**
   - **Gratitude Journaling:**
   - Maintain a gratitude journal to regularly record things you are thankful for. Reflecting on positive aspects of life enhances a sense of appreciation and redirects focus from stressors to the positive elements that contribute to well-being.
   - **Three Good Things Exercise:**
   - Each day, identify three positive events or experiences. Reflect on the role you played in these positive occurrences. This exercise promotes a positive mindset by emphasizing personal agency and recognizing the positive aspects of daily life.
   - **Strengths Identification:**
   - Take time to identify and acknowledge your strengths.
     Utilize tools like the VIA Survey of Character Strengths to identify your signature strengths. Embracing and applying these strengths in daily life contributes to a sense of competence and resilience against stress.

- **Random Acts of Kindness:**
- Engage in random acts of kindness toward others. Acts of generosity, no matter how small, contribute to a sense of connection and purpose. The positive impact on others and the community fosters a more optimistic and fulfilling perspective.
- **Mindfulness-Based Gratitude Meditation:**
- Combine mindfulness with gratitude by practicing a gratitude meditation. Focus on the sensations of gratitude in the body and mind, cultivating a deep sense of appreciation. This practice enhances mindfulness and promotes a positive outlook.
- **Positive Affirmations:**
- Create and repeat positive affirmations that resonate with your goals and values. Affirmations help challenge negative self-talk and cultivate a more optimistic and empowering internal dialogue, influencing the perception of stressors.

5. **Acceptance and Commitment Therapy (ACT):**
   - Embrace principles of ACT, which involve accepting the presence of stress without judgment and committing to actions aligned with personal values. By acknowledging and allowing stress to coexist while taking intentional steps toward valued goals, individuals can transform their relationship with stress.

6. **Reframing Stress as a Challenge:**
   - **Cognitive Restructuring Exercises:**
   - Engage in cognitive restructuring by identifying and challenging negative thoughts associated with stress. Reframe stress-inducing thoughts to emphasize the potential for growth and learning. This exercise contributes to a more constructive perception of challenges.
   - **Goal Setting and Planning:**
   - Set specific and achievable goals when faced with stressors. Break down larger challenges into smaller, manageable steps. Planning and setting milestones create a roadmap, transforming stress into a series of achievable tasks.
   - **Mindful Problem-Solving:**
   - Approach stressors with a mindful problem-solving mindset. Instead of reacting impulsively, take a step back, assess the situation, and consider possible solutions. Mindful problem-solving promotes a proactive and strategic approach to challenges.
   - **Learning Mindset Reflection:**
   - Reflect on stressors with a learning mindset. Ask yourself what lessons or insights can be gained from the challenges you face. Embracing a mindset focused on continuous learning contributes to resilience and personal development.
   - **Daily Growth Journal:**
   - Maintain a growth journal where you document instances of personal growth and lessons learned from challenging experiences. Regularly review and celebrate your progress, reinforcing the idea that challenges contribute to your development.
   - **Self-Efficacy Building:**
   - Cultivate self-efficacy by intentionally taking on challenges and setting achievable goals.

7. **Perspective-Taking Exercises:**
   - Engage in perspective-taking exercises to broaden understanding. Consider alternative viewpoints and potential positive outcomes associated with stressors. This practice cultivates empathy and helps individuals reframe their perspective on stress-inducing situations.

8. **Humor and Laughter Therapy:**
   - Integrate humor and laughter into daily life to alter the perception of stress. Laughter triggers the release of endorphins, promoting a positive mood and diminishing the physiological effects of stress. Finding humor in challenging situations enhances resilience.

9. **Gratitude Practices:**
   - Cultivate gratitude as a means of shifting focus from stressors to positive aspects of life. Regularly express thanks for small and significant elements of life through practices like gratitude journaling, creating a positive feedback loop that influences perception.

10. **Narrative Reframing:**
    - Explore narrative reframing by altering the storytelling around stressors.
    Instead of viewing challenges as insurmountable, construct narratives that emphasize personal growth, resilience, and the ability to overcome adversity. This narrative shift shapes a more empowering perception of stress.

11. **Flow State Engagement:**
    - Immerse yourself in activities that induce a state of flow—complete absorption and enjoyment in a task. When in a flow state, individuals often lose track of time and experience a sense of fulfillment, altering their perception of stress and promoting a more positive mindset.
12. **Mindful Self-Compassion:**
    - **Loving-Kindness Meditation for Self:**
    - Incorporate loving-kindness meditation specifically directed towards oneself. Repeat phrases such as "May I be happy, may I be healthy, may I be at ease." This practice fosters a sense of self-compassion and warmth during stressful moments.
    - **Self-Compassion Breaks:**
    - Integrate self-compassion breaks into your day.
      When feeling stressed, take a few moments to acknowledge the difficulty, recognize that it's a shared human experience, and offer yourself words of kindness. This brief practice can shift your perspective on stress.
    - **Self-Compassion Journaling:**
    - Keep a self-compassion journal to document your thoughts and feelings during stressful times. Write down compassionate and understanding responses to your own struggles. This reflective practice reinforces the habit of treating yourself with kindness.
    - **Affirmations of Self-Kindness:**
    - Develop and repeat affirmations that emphasize self-kindness during stress. For instance, "I am deserving of compassion," or "I treat myself with gentleness in challenging moments." Consistent repetition strengthens the internal dialogue of self-compassion.
13. **Strengths-Based Approach:**
    - Adopt a strengths-based approach by focusing on personal strengths and capabilities when facing stressors.
      Identifying and utilizing strengths contributes to a sense of competence and self-efficacy, influencing how stress is perceived and managed.
14. **Visualization Techniques:**
    - **Progressive Desensitization:**
    - Gradually expose yourself to stressors in your imagination, starting with less challenging scenarios and progressing to more complex ones. This technique helps desensitize the fear response and builds confidence in your ability to face and overcome stressors.
    - **Future Self-Visualization:**
    - Imagine your future self successfully navigating and overcoming stressors. Visualize the qualities, skills, and mindset your future self possesses. This visualization fosters a sense of empowerment and provides a positive image to aspire to.
    - **Outcome Visualization:**
    - Envision the positive outcomes of successfully managing stressors. Picture the sense of accomplishment, relief, and personal growth associated with overcoming challenges.

The Art of Saying No:
Setting Boundaries

1. **Self-Reflection on Priorities:**
   - **Vision Board for Priorities:**
   - Create a vision board that visually represents your core values and priorities. Use images, words, and symbols that resonate with what matters most to you. Display the board as a daily reminder to align your choices with your identified priorities.
   - **Values Clarification Exercises:**
   - Engage in values clarification exercises to articulate and prioritize your core values. Various worksheets and prompts are available to guide this process. This clarity empowers you to make decisions that honor your values and set appropriate boundaries.
   - **Life Wheel Assessment:**
   - Use a life wheel assessment tool to evaluate various aspects of your life, such as career, relationships, health, and personal growth. This visual representation helps identify areas where boundaries may be needed and allows for intentional adjustments.
   - **Time Audit and Prioritization:**
   - Conduct a time audit to assess how you currently spend your time. Identify activities that align with your priorities and those that do not. Prioritize tasks and commitments based on their significance to your values, allowing for more intentional boundary-setting.
   - **Periodic Goal Review:**
   - Schedule regular reviews of your short-term and long-term goals. Assess whether your current commitments align with these goals. Adjustments may be necessary to ensure that your actions and decisions support your overarching objectives.
2. **Clarity in Communication:**
   - Practice clear and assertive communication when expressing your boundaries. Clearly articulate your needs, limitations, and priorities without ambiguity. Being direct helps others understand your position and expectations.
3. **Understanding Your Capacity:**
   - Assess your current workload, commitments, and energy levels before agreeing to new tasks or responsibilities.
     Being aware of your capacity enables you to make informed decisions about what you can realistically take on without overwhelming yourself.
4. **Prioritization Techniques:**
   - **Time Blocking:**
   - Implement time blocking to allocate specific blocks of time to different categories of tasks. Designate time for high-priority, important tasks, and establish boundaries around those time blocks to avoid distractions.
   - **Mind Mapping for Prioritization:**
   - Create mind maps to visually represent tasks, projects, and goals. This technique helps identify key priorities and their interconnectedness. By visualizing the relationships between tasks, you can make more informed decisions about where to focus your efforts.
   - **Weekly Priority Setting Ritual:**
   - Establish a weekly ritual for setting priorities. At the beginning of each week, review your goals and commitments. Use this dedicated time to identify the most important tasks and set realistic priorities for the upcoming week.
   - **Collaborative Priority Discussions:**
   - Engage in collaborative priority discussions with team members, colleagues, or family members. Aligning priorities collectively fosters a shared understanding of what matters most. This collaboration can lead to more effective distribution of responsibilities and shared goals.
   - **Mindful Prioritization Meditation:**
   - Practice a mindful prioritization meditation. During this meditation, focus on your breathing and then bring your attention to your tasks. Allow thoughts of priorities to arise naturally, and

observe them without judgment. This mindfulness practice can enhance clarity in decision-making.

5. **Practice Saying No Politely:**
   - **Positive Reframing:**
   - Reframe your no with a positive tone. Instead of a straightforward decline, express gratitude for the opportunity and provide a brief explanation of your current commitments. For instance, "Thank you for considering me. Unfortunately, my plate is quite full right now."
   - **Offer Alternatives:**
   - Soften the no by offering alternatives when possible. If you cannot commit to a specific request, suggest an alternative solution or recommend someone who may be better suited for the task. This approach demonstrates your willingness to help despite your inability to say yes.
   - **Time-Bound Responses:**
   - Set a time boundary for responding to requests. If unsure about committing, let the requester know that you need time to check your schedule or assess your workload. This buys you the necessary time to make an informed decision and respond assertively.
   - **Firm Body Language and Tone:**
   - Practice assertive body language and tone when delivering a polite no. Maintain eye contact, stand or sit upright, and use a calm but firm voice. Assertiveness in non-verbal communication reinforces the sincerity of your response.
   - **Scripting No Responses:**
   - Develop scripted responses for common scenarios where you need to say no.
     Having pre-prepared phrases allows you to respond confidently and politely in the moment. For example, "I appreciate your invitation, but unfortunately, I won't be able to commit due to prior obligations."

6. **Setting Clear Expectations:**
   - **Establishing Communication Channels:**
   - Clearly define preferred communication channels and response times. Communicate whether certain matters are more suitable for emails, meetings, or instant messaging. Setting these expectations aids in managing communication overload.
   - **Creating a Professional Boundaries Document:**
   - Develop a document outlining your professional boundaries. Include information about your working hours, preferred communication methods, and any specific limitations you may have. Share this document with colleagues and collaborators to ensure clarity.
   - **Utilizing Out-of-Office Messages Effectively:**
   - Use out-of-office messages strategically to communicate your availability. Clearly state your current commitments, when you will be available again, and provide alternative contacts if necessary.
   - **Consistent Communication of Boundaries:**
   - Regularly reinforce your boundaries through consistent communication. Remind colleagues and collaborators about your working hours, availability, and any specific limitations. This ongoing reinforcement helps establish a culture of respect for boundaries.
   - **Team Agreement on Work Norms:**
   - Collaborate with team members to create a collective agreement on work norms and boundaries. This could involve discussions about response times, meeting schedules, and expectations for after-hours work. Mutual agreement fosters a supportive work environment.
   - **Incorporating Boundaries into Project Planning:**
   - When involved in project planning or team assignments, integrate discussions about individual boundaries. Consider factors such as preferred working hours, potential periods of unavailability, and the need for breaks. Proactively addressing boundaries can prevent future conflicts.

7. **Learn to Delegate:**
   - Delegate tasks when possible, especially in professional and personal settings.
     Delegating empowers others and allows you to focus on high-priority responsibilities, reducing the overall burden on your time and energy.

8. **Establishing Personal Time Blocks:**
   - Schedule dedicated blocks of personal time in your calendar. Whether it's for relaxation, hobbies, or self-care, treating personal time as non-negotiable reinforces the importance of maintaining a balanced life and helps you resist overcommitting.
9. **Self-Advocacy Skills:**
   - : Develop self-advocacy skills to express your needs confidently. This involves recognizing when a request or commitment goes against your boundaries and having the ability to assertively communicate your position.
10. **Mindfulness in Decision-Making:**
    - Practice mindfulness when making decisions about commitments. Before saying yes, take a moment to check in with yourself and assess whether the request aligns with your priorities and well-being. Mindful decision-making enhances awareness of potential stressors.
11. **Establishing Work-Life Balance:**
    - **Digital Detox Rituals:**
    - Implement regular digital detox rituals, especially during personal time. Designate specific periods, such as evenings or weekends, for disconnecting from work-related emails, messages, and notifications. This practice fosters a healthier balance between professional and personal life.
    - **Create a Designated Workspace:**
    - Designate a specific area for work-related activities. When in this space, focus on work tasks, and when outside of it, prioritize personal and leisure activities. This physical boundary helps reinforce the separation between work and personal life.
    - **Mindful Transition Practices:**
    - Develop mindful transition practices to signal the end of the workday and the beginning of personal time. This could involve a brief mindfulness meditation, a short walk, or a ritual that helps shift your mindset away from work-related concerns.
    - **Set Realistic Work Hours:**
    - Establish realistic and sustainable work hours that align with your energy levels and personal commitments. Avoid consistently working extended hours, as this can lead to burnout and a skewed work-life balance.
12. **Progressive Boundary Setting:**
    - Gradually implement boundaries rather than making drastic changes overnight. This progressive approach allows you to assess the impact of each boundary and adjust as needed, making the adjustment more manageable for both you and others.
13. **Confidence in Prioritizing Self-Care:**
    - Cultivate confidence in prioritizing self-care and personal well-being. Recognize that saying no to certain commitments is a proactive step toward maintaining balance and preventing burnout.
14. **Setting Technology Boundaries:**
    - Establish boundaries with technology to prevent constant connectivity-related stress. Consider implementing specific time frames for checking emails or messages, reducing notifications, and designating tech-free zones during personal time.
15. **Seeking Support in Boundary Setting:**
    - Seek support from mentors, colleagues, or friends in navigating and setting boundaries.

Chapter 3

Simplify to Amplify:
Decluttering Your Life

1. **Minimalism Mindset:**
   - Embrace a minimalist mindset by focusing on what truly adds value to your life. Minimalism is not just about physical possessions but extends to relationships, commitments, and digital spaces. Assess each aspect of your life, keeping only what aligns with your priorities.
2. **Physical Decluttering:**
   - **Minimalist Wardrobe Challenge:**
   - Embark on a minimalist wardrobe challenge. Assess your clothing items and create a capsule wardrobe with versatile pieces. Donate or discard items you haven't worn in a while. A streamlined wardrobe simplifies decision-making and reduces clutter.
   - **One-In, One-Out Rule:**
   - Implement the one-in, one-out rule for new belongings. For every new item you bring into your living or working space, commit to removing one existing item. This practice prevents accumulation and encourages mindful consumption.
   - **Decluttering Sessions:**
   - Schedule regular decluttering sessions for specific areas of your home or workspace. Set aside dedicated time to assess and organize belongings, ensuring that clutter does not accumulate over time.
   - **Digital Decluttering:**
   - Extend decluttering to your digital life. Organize files, folders, and emails, deleting unnecessary items. Clear your digital workspace to enhance efficiency and reduce mental clutter associated with digital disorganization.
   - **Visual Cues for Organization:**
   - Use visual cues for organization. Invest in storage solutions such as baskets, shelves, and containers to keep items in designated places. Clearly labeled storage helps maintain order and simplifies the process of finding what you need.
3. **One-In, One-Out Rule:**
   - Implement the one-in, one-out rule for possessions. For every new item you bring into your life, consider letting go of an existing one. This helps maintain a balanced and clutter-free environment, preventing accumulation.
4. **Digital Detox:**
   - **Social Media Sabbaticals:**
   - Plan periodic social media sabbaticals. Take intentional breaks from social media platforms to reduce the constant influx of information. Use this time to focus on real-life interactions, hobbies, or personal development.
   - **Unsubscribe and Unfollow:**
   - Regularly review your email subscriptions and social media accounts. Unsubscribe from newsletters or unfollow accounts that no longer provide value or align with your interests. This minimizes digital clutter and ensures your feeds are curated to your preferences.
   - **App Notification Management:**
   - Customize app notifications on your devices. Disable non-essential notifications to reduce interruptions and maintain better focus. Prioritize notifications from essential apps, allowing for a more intentional use of technology.
   - **Digital Sabbath Days:**
   - Designate specific days as digital Sabbath days. On these days, disconnect from electronic devices, including smartphones, tablets, and computers.
     Engage in analog activities such as reading physical books, spending time outdoors, or enjoying face-to-face interactions.
   - **Email Management Strategies:**

- Implement effective email management strategies. Use filters and folders to categorize emails, archive or delete outdated messages, and respond promptly to important communications. Adopting organized email practices reduces the sense of digital overwhelm.

5. **Mindful Consumption:**
   - Adopt mindful consumption habits. Before making a purchase, ask yourself if it aligns with your needs and values. Avoid impulsive buying, and focus on acquiring items that truly contribute to your well-being.

6. **Time Audit for Commitments:**
   - Conduct a time audit to assess your commitments and activities. Identify those that align with your priorities and bring fulfillment. Eliminate or delegate tasks that do not contribute positively to your life.

7. **Unsubscribe and Unfollow:**
   - **Activity:** Unsubscribe from email lists and unfollow social media accounts that do not add value or align with your interests.
   Streamlining your digital content reduces information overwhelm and fosters a more intentional online experience.

8. **Evaluate Relationships:**
   - **Reflective Relationship Journal:**
   - Keep a reflective journal dedicated to your relationships. Note your feelings, observations, and the overall impact each relationship has on your well-being. Regular reflection helps identify patterns and assess the health of your connections.
   - **Communication Transparency:**
   - Practice transparent communication in your relationships. Share your thoughts, feelings, and expectations openly, and encourage others to do the same. This transparency fosters understanding and helps maintain healthy connections.
   - **Mindful Listening Practices:**
   - Develop mindful listening practices in your interactions. Actively listen to others without immediately formulating responses. This cultivates a deeper understanding of your relationships and promotes more meaningful connections.
   - **Relationship Inventory:**
   - Conduct a relationship inventory by listing the key people in your life. Evaluate the nature of each relationship, assessing whether it contributes positively or presents challenges. This inventory aids in prioritizing connections that align with your well-being.
   - **Boundaries in Relationships:**
   - Establish clear boundaries in your relationships. Communicate your needs and expectations, and respect the boundaries of others. Healthy boundaries contribute to balanced and respectful interactions.

9. **Streamline Daily Routines:**
   - Streamline your daily routines to minimize decision fatigue. Simplify choices such as clothing selection, meal planning, and morning rituals. This reduces stress and frees up mental energy for more meaningful decisions.

10. **Mindful Time Blocking:**
    - **Deep Work Sessions:**
    - Dedicate specific time blocks for deep work sessions. During these periods, eliminate distractions and focus entirely on high-priority, cognitively demanding tasks.
    Deep work enhances productivity and allows for more meaningful accomplishments.
    - **Technology-Free Blocks:**
    - Create technology-free time blocks to reduce digital distractions. Turn off notifications and set designated periods where you disconnect from electronic devices. This fosters mindfulness, minimizes information overload, and promotes a sense of presence in the moment.
    - **Morning Ritual Blocks:**
    - Establish morning ritual blocks to set a positive tone for the day. Include activities such as meditation, exercise, or journaling to create a mindful and intentional start. These rituals contribute to overall well-being and mental clarity.
    - **Energy Management Blocks:**

- Schedule time blocks based on your energy levels. Identify periods of the day when your energy is highest for focused work and reserve those times for tasks requiring concentration. Align less demanding activities with lower energy periods.
- **Batch Processing Communication:**
- Allocate specific time blocks for communication-related tasks. Instead of responding to emails and messages throughout the day, batch process these activities during designated periods. This prevents constant interruptions and allows for more focused communication.

11. **Declutter Mental Noise:**
    - Declutter mental noise through mindfulness and meditation. Take time each day for mindfulness exercises to quiet the mind, reduce stress, and gain clarity. Mindful practices contribute to a more balanced and focused mental state.

12. **Financial Simplification:**
    - Simplify your finances by consolidating accounts, automating bill payments, and creating a budget. A clear financial picture reduces stress and allows for a more intentional use of resources.

13. **Regular Life Assessments:**
    - Conduct regular life assessments to evaluate your goals, values, and aspirations. Adjust your path based on changing priorities, and eliminate activities or commitments that no longer align with your evolving life vision.

14. **Mindful Eating Habits:**
    - Practice mindful eating by simplifying your approach to meals. Focus on whole, nutritious foods and savor each bite. Avoid excessive choices that can lead to decision fatigue and prioritize nourishing your body.

15. **Digital Mindfulness Practices:**
    - Incorporate digital mindfulness practices, such as limiting screen time before bedtime and creating designated tech-free zones. This helps in reducing the impact of constant digital stimulation on your overall well-being.

16. **Gratitude Journaling for Abundance:**
    - Keep a gratitude journal to shift your focus from what you lack to what you have. Regularly note the things you are grateful for, fostering a mindset of abundance and contentment.

17. **Learn to Say No:**
    - Cultivate the ability to say no gracefully. Assess your commitments and obligations, and decline those that do not align with your priorities or contribute positively to your life.

18. **Create White Space:**
    - Intentionally create white space in your schedule – periods of time with no planned activities. This provides flexibility, reduces stress, and allows for spontaneous moments of joy or relaxation.

19. **Mindful Travel Planning:**
    - Apply mindfulness to travel planning by focusing on experiences that align with your interests and values. Avoid overloading your itinerary and allow for moments of spontaneity and relaxation during your travels.

20. **Regular Life Detox Days:**
    - Dedicate regular life detox days where you intentionally step back from routine obligations. Use these days for reflection, self-care, and activities that bring joy. This periodic reset contributes to a more balanced and fulfilling life.

Nutrition and Stress:
Eating for a Calmer You

1. **Balanced Diet Basics:**
   - Prioritize a balanced diet that includes a variety of food groups, such as fruits, vegetables, whole grains, lean proteins, and healthy fats. This provides essential nutrients that support overall well-being and contribute to stress management.
2. **Hydration for Stress Relief:**
   - **Electrolyte Balance:**
   - Ensure a balance of electrolytes in your hydration routine. Include sources of electrolytes such as potassium, magnesium, and sodium, which play a crucial role in maintaining proper fluid balance and supporting stress reduction.
   - **Coconut Water for Natural Hydration:**
   - Incorporate coconut water as a natural and hydrating alternative. Coconut water is rich in electrolytes and can provide a refreshing and replenishing drink, aiding in hydration and stress relief.
   - **Timing of Hydration:**
   - Pay attention to the timing of your hydration.
     Start your day with a glass of water, and maintain consistent hydration throughout the day. Avoid excessive consumption close to bedtime to promote uninterrupted sleep.
   - **Herbal Infusions for Relaxation:**
   - Experiment with herbal infusions known for their calming properties. Chamomile, lavender, and peppermint teas are examples of herbal drinks that not only contribute to hydration but also offer relaxation benefits.
   - **Incorporate Hydrating Foods:**
   - Integrate hydrating foods into your diet. Water-rich fruits and vegetables, such as watermelon, cucumber, and oranges, not only contribute to overall hydration but also provide essential vitamins and minerals for stress management.
3. **Mindful Eating Practices:**
   - Practice mindful eating to enhance the connection between food and emotions. Pay attention to the colors, textures, and flavors of your meals. Eating slowly and savoring each bite helps prevent overeating and promotes a more mindful approach to nourishment.
4. **Complex Carbohydrates for Stability:**
   - Include complex carbohydrates in your diet, such as whole grains, brown rice, and legumes. These foods release energy slowly, helping stabilize blood sugar levels and providing a consistent source of fuel for both the body and brain.
5. **Omega-3 Fatty Acids for Brain Health:**
   - Incorporate omega-3 fatty acids into your diet through sources like fatty fish (salmon, mackerel), flaxseeds, chia seeds, and walnuts. Omega-3s are known to support brain health and may have a positive impact on mood regulation.
6. **Protein for Sustained Energy:**
   - **Diverse Protein Sources:**
   - Incorporate a variety of protein sources into your diet. Include options such as lean meats, poultry, fish, tofu, tempeh, legumes, beans, and lentils. This ensures a diverse nutrient profile and adds culinary variety to your meals.
   - **Plant-Based Protein Alternatives:**
   - Explore plant-based protein alternatives, especially if you follow a vegetarian or vegan diet.
   - **Balanced Protein Intake:**
   - Strive for a balanced distribution of protein throughout the day. Include protein in each meal to support stable blood sugar levels and provide a steady release of energy. Avoid heavily relying on one meal for the majority of your daily protein intake.

- **Protein Snacking:**
- Opt for protein-rich snacks to maintain energy levels between meals. Greek yogurt, cottage cheese, nuts, and seeds make convenient and nutritious snack options that can help prevent energy dips and promote overall satiety.
- **Pre-Workout Protein:**
- Consume a protein-rich snack before engaging in physical activities. This provides the necessary amino acids for muscle support and helps sustain energy during workouts. Consider options like a protein smoothie or a small serving of chicken with vegetables.

7. **Limit Caffeine and Sugar Intake:**
   - Moderate your consumption of caffeine and refined sugars.
     Excessive caffeine can contribute to increased anxiety, while refined sugars may lead to energy spikes and crashes. Opt for alternatives like herbal teas and choose natural sweeteners like honey or maple syrup.

8. **Nutrient-Rich Snacking:**
   - Choose nutrient-rich snacks to maintain energy levels between meals. Snack on fruits, vegetables, nuts, or yogurt to provide your body with essential vitamins and minerals without the added sugars and artificial ingredients found in many processed snacks.

9. **Adaptogenic Herbs:**
   - Explore adaptogenic herbs like ashwagandha, rhodiola, and holy basil, known for their potential stress-relieving properties. Consult with a healthcare professional before incorporating these supplements, especially if you have existing health conditions or are taking medications.

10. **Prebiotics and Probiotics for Gut Health:**
    - Support gut health with prebiotics (found in foods like garlic, onions, bananas) and probiotics (fermented foods like yogurt, kefir, sauerkraut). The gut-brain connection suggests that a healthy gut contributes to improved mood and stress resilience.

11. **Vitamin-Rich Foods:**
    - **Complex Carbohydrates for Mood Stability:**
    - Incorporate complex carbohydrates into your diet, such as whole grains, brown rice, and oats. These foods release glucose slowly, providing a steady supply of energy and stabilizing mood. Avoid excessive refined sugars, as they can contribute to energy crashes and irritability.
    - **Omega-3 Fatty Acids for Brain Health:**
    - Include sources of omega-3 fatty acids in your diet, such as fatty fish (salmon, mackerel), flaxseeds, and walnuts. Omega-3s support brain health and have been associated with reducing symptoms of stress and anxiety.
    - **Probiotics for Gut-Brain Connection:**
    - Consume foods rich in probiotics, such as yogurt, kefir, and fermented vegetables. The gut-brain connection plays a crucial role in stress management, and a healthy gut microbiome can positively impact mood and resilience to stress.
    - **Magnesium-Rich Foods for Relaxation:**
    - Incorporate magnesium-rich foods into your diet, including leafy greens, nuts, seeds, and whole grains.
      Magnesium has relaxing properties and may help alleviate symptoms of stress by supporting muscle and nerve function.
    - **Herbal Teas for Calming Rituals:**
    - Include herbal teas known for their calming properties in your routine. Chamomile, lavender, and valerian root teas can contribute to relaxation and support a calm state of mind. Enjoying these teas as part of a calming ritual can enhance their stress-relieving effects.

12. **Incorporate Magnesium:**
    - Include magnesium-rich foods such as leafy green vegetables, nuts, seeds, and whole grains. Magnesium plays a role in muscle relaxation and may contribute to a sense of calmness.

13. **Turmeric and Anti-Inflammatory Foods:**
    - **Ginger for Digestive Health:**
    - Incorporate ginger into your diet to support digestive health. Ginger has anti-inflammatory properties and may help alleviate digestive discomfort, promoting overall well-being.
    - **Colorful Vegetables for a Nutrient Boost:**
    - Include a variety of colorful vegetables in your meals.

Vegetables like bell peppers, tomatoes, and leafy greens contain a range of antioxidants and phytochemicals that combat inflammation and support overall health.

- **Omega-3-Rich Fish for Joint Health:**
- Consume fatty fish rich in omega-3 fatty acids, such as salmon and mackerel. Omega-3s have anti-inflammatory effects and may benefit joint health, reducing discomfort associated with inflammation.
- **Green Tea for Polyphenols:**
- Enjoy green tea as a beverage rich in polyphenols. Polyphenols have antioxidant and anti-inflammatory properties that may contribute to reducing oxidative stress in the body.
- **Dark Leafy Greens for Vitamin K:**
- Include dark leafy greens like kale and spinach in your meals. These greens are high in vitamin K, which has anti-inflammatory effects and supports bone health.

14. **Meal Planning and Preparation:**
   - Plan and prepare meals in advance to avoid reliance on fast food or processed snacks.
   Having nutritious meals readily available reduces decision fatigue and supports consistent, healthy eating habits.

15. **Seek Professional Guidance:**
   - **Comprehensive Nutritional Assessment:**
   - Schedule a comprehensive nutritional assessment with a registered dietitian or nutritionist. This assessment involves a detailed review of your dietary habits, lifestyle, and health goals. Professionals can identify areas for improvement and develop a personalized plan to address your specific needs.
   - **Identifying Dietary Triggers:**
   - Work with a professional to identify potential dietary triggers that may contribute to stress. Some individuals may have sensitivities or allergies to certain foods that can impact mood and overall well-being. A thorough assessment can help pinpoint and address these triggers.
   - **Balancing Macronutrients:**
   - Receive guidance on achieving a balanced intake of macronutrients (carbohydrates, proteins, and fats).
   A professional can help tailor your macronutrient ratios based on your lifestyle, activity level, and stress management goals.
   - **Individualized Meal Planning:**
   - Collaborate with a nutrition expert to create individualized meal plans that align with your stress management objectives. These plans can incorporate a variety of nutrient-dense foods, ensuring you receive essential vitamins and minerals to support overall well-being.
   - **Supplementation Guidance:**
   - If necessary, explore the possibility of incorporating dietary supplements under the guidance of a professional. They can assess whether specific vitamins, minerals, or other supplements may be beneficial for stress management based on your unique nutritional needs.

Part Three:
Mindfulness and Awareness

Mindfulness 101: Living in the Present

1. **Understanding Mindfulness:**
   - Mindfulness involves being fully present in the current moment without judgment. It's the practice of intentionally paying attention to your thoughts, emotions, and sensations, fostering a heightened awareness of your surroundings and inner experiences.
2. **Mindful Breathing Techniques:**
   - **Body Scan Meditation:**
   - Practice body scan meditation to cultivate awareness of bodily sensations. Start from your toes and gradually move up to your head, paying attention to each part of your body. This technique enhances mindfulness by grounding you in the present moment.
   - **Mindful Walking:**
   - Engage in mindful walking to bring attention to each step and the sensations in your body as you move. Focus on the connection between your feet and the ground. This simple yet powerful practice can be incorporated into daily walks or even short breaks during the day.
   - **Five Senses Check-In:**
   - Perform a five senses check-in to anchor yourself in the present. Notice five things you can see, four things you can touch, three things you can hear, two things you can smell, and one thing you can taste. This exercise promotes sensory awareness and presence.
   - **Mindful Eating:**
   - Practice mindful eating by savoring each bite without distractions. Pay attention to the taste, texture, and aroma of your food. This technique not only enhances the eating experience but also fosters a connection with the present moment.
   - **Daily Mindfulness Reminders:**
   - Set reminders throughout the day to pause and practice mindfulness. Use cues like the chime of a bell, the vibration of your phone, or specific events (e.g., opening a door) to bring your attention to the present moment regularly.
   - **Gratitude Journaling:**
   - Keep a gratitude journal to reflect on and appreciate the positive aspects of your life. Regularly noting things you are grateful for fosters a mindful acknowledgment of the present blessings, promoting a positive mindset.
3. **Body Scan Meditation:**
   - Engage in body scan meditations to cultivate awareness of physical sensations. Begin at one end of your body and progressively move attention through each body part, noticing any tension or relaxation. This practice enhances bodily awareness and promotes relaxation.
4. **Mindful Walking:**
   - Incorporate mindful walking into your routine. Pay attention to each step, the sensation of your feet connecting with the ground, and the movement of your body. This practice brings mindfulness into everyday activities, grounding you in the present moment.
5. **Observing Thoughts and Emotions:**
   - Practice observing your thoughts and emotions without attachment or judgment. Imagine them as passing clouds in the sky; acknowledge their presence, but let them drift away. This non-reactive awareness promotes a more balanced perspective on your internal experiences.
6. **Mindful Eating:**
   - **Practice:** Transform mealtime into a mindful experience.
     Pay attention to the colors, textures, and flavors of your food. Chew slowly and savor each bite. Mindful eating fosters a deeper connection with your meals and prevents mindless consumption.

7. **Daily Mindfulness Rituals:**
   - **Mindful Morning Routine:**
   - Infuse mindfulness into your morning routine. Whether it's brushing your teeth, washing your face, or making your bed, approach each activity with full attention to the sensations and movements involved. This sets a positive tone for the day.
   - **Mindful Tea or Coffee Time:**
   - Transform your tea or coffee-drinking ritual into a mindful experience. Focus on the aroma, temperature, and taste of each sip. Allow this moment to be a calming and intentional start to your day.
   - **Mindful Commuting:**
   - Turn your commute into a mindfulness practice. Whether walking, cycling, or driving, pay attention to the sights, sounds, and sensations around you. Use this time to center yourself before reaching your destination.
   - **Mindful Meal Preparation:**
   - Engage in mindful meal preparation. Pay attention to the colors, textures, and smells of the ingredients. Be present as you chop, cook, and assemble your meals, turning the process into a meditative and enjoyable activity.
   - **Mindful Eating Practices:**
   - Extend mindfulness to your meals by savoring each bite. Chew slowly, pay attention to flavors, and put down your utensils between bites. This mindful eating practice enhances the pleasure of dining and encourages a more conscious approach to nourishment.

8. **Mindfulness Apps and Resources:**
   - Explore mindfulness apps and resources that offer guided meditations and exercises. Apps like Headspace, Calm, or Insight Timer provide structured sessions to help you develop and sustain a mindfulness practice.

9. **Mindful Journaling:**
   - Incorporate mindful journaling into your routine.
     Reflect on your thoughts, feelings, and experiences, observing them without judgment. This practice enhances self-awareness and allows for the release of pent-up emotions.

10. **Mindfulness in Stressful Situations:**
    - **Mindful Breathing Breaks:**
    - During stressful moments, take short mindful breathing breaks. Step away if possible, close your eyes, and focus on deep, intentional breaths. This brief pause can provide clarity and calmness.
    - **Mindful Grounding Techniques:**
    - Use grounding techniques during stress. Focus on the sensations of your body against a surface, the feeling of your breath, or the awareness of your surroundings. This anchors you in the present moment during challenging situations.
    - **Mindful Observation of Thoughts:**
    - When stress arises, practice observing your thoughts without judgment. Allow them to come and go like passing clouds. This mindfulness of thoughts reduces attachment to stressful thinking patterns.
    - **Mindful Body Scan:**
    - Conduct a quick mindful body scan during stress. Start from your toes and progressively move up, noting any tension or discomfort. This brings attention to your body and helps release physical tension.
    - **Mindful Sensory Awareness:**
    - Engage your senses mindfully in stressful situations. Notice the sights, sounds, smells, and tactile sensations around you. This sensory awareness can shift your focus away from stressors.

11. **Mindfulness-Based Stress Reduction (MBSR):**
    - Consider enrolling in a Mindfulness-Based Stress Reduction program. MBSR programs, often available in-person or online, offer structured guidance in developing mindfulness skills and integrating them into various aspects of life.

12. **Mindful Communication:**
    - Bring mindfulness into your communication. Listen attentively to others, fully engaging in the conversation without formulating your response. Mindful communication fosters deeper connections and understanding in relationships.
13. **Gratitude and Mindfulness:**
    - **Gratitude Meditation:**
    - Integrate gratitude into mindfulness meditation. During your meditation sessions, focus on feelings of gratitude. Cultivate a sense of appreciation for the present moment, your breath, and the opportunities life offers.
    - **Gratitude Walks:**
    - Take gratitude walks where you mindfully appreciate your surroundings. Notice the beauty in nature, architecture, or even the bustling energy of a city. Express gratitude for the ability to experience these moments.
    - **Mindful Gratitude Journaling:**
    - Combine mindfulness with gratitude journaling. Set aside dedicated time to reflect on the positive aspects of your day. Mindfully recount moments of gratitude, noting specific details and emotions associated with each.
    - **Gratitude Affirmations:**
    - Use gratitude affirmations during mindful breathing exercises.
    Inhale positive affirmations related to gratitude and exhale any tension or negativity. This practice combines the benefits of mindful breathing with a focus on gratitude.
14. **Mindfulness Retreats:**
    - Consider attending mindfulness retreats for immersive experiences. These retreats offer dedicated time to deepen your mindfulness practice in a supportive environment, away from daily distractions.
15. **Mindfulness and Sleep:**
    - Develop a mindfulness routine before bedtime to improve sleep quality. Engage in relaxation techniques, mindful breathing, or gentle stretches to create a calming transition from the day to restful sleep.
16. **Mindfulness and Creative Expression:**
    - Channel mindfulness into creative pursuits. Engage in activities like painting, writing, or playing music with full attention. Creative expression becomes a meditative process, allowing for self-discovery and stress relief.
17. **Mindfulness and Acceptance:**
    - Embrace the principle of acceptance in mindfulness. Acknowledge that not every moment will be stress-free, but through mindfulness, you can accept and navigate challenges with greater resilience.
18. **Mindful Technology Use:**
    - Cultivate awareness when using technology. Practice mindful scrolling by paying attention to content and the impact it has on your mood. Set intentional limits to prevent excessive screen time, fostering a more mindful relationship with technology.
19. **Mindfulness and Nature Connection:**
    - Spend time in nature with a mindful approach. Observe the sights, sounds, and sensations of the natural environment. Nature connection enhances mindfulness and provides a grounding experience.
20. **Mindfulness and Compassion:**
    - Integrate mindfulness with self-compassion. Be kind to yourself during challenging moments, acknowledging that everyone faces difficulties. Mindfulness combined with self-compassion promotes emotional resilience and well-being.

Breathing Techniques
for Immediate Relief

1. **Diaphragmatic Breathing (Deep Belly Breathing):**
   * Sit or lie down comfortably. Place one hand on your chest and the other on your abdomen. Inhale deeply through your nose, allowing your diaphragm to expand and your abdomen to rise. Exhale slowly through pursed lips, feeling your abdomen fall. Repeat for several breaths.
   * Diaphragmatic breathing activates the body's relaxation response, reducing stress and promoting a sense of calmness.

2. **Box Breathing (Square Breathing):**
   * **Deep Abdominal Breathing:**
   * Inhale deeply through your nose, allowing your diaphragm to expand. Feel your abdomen rise as you fill your lungs with air. Exhale slowly and completely through your mouth, feeling your abdomen fall. Repeat this deep breathing pattern for several cycles.
   * Deep abdominal breathing activates the body's relaxation response, reducing stress hormones and promoting a sense of calm.
   * **Alternate Nostril Breathing (Nadi Shodhana):**
   * Sit comfortably and use your thumb and ring finger to alternate blocking one nostril at a time. Inhale deeply through one nostril, then exhale through the other. Continue this pattern, switching nostrils with each breath.
   * Nadi Shodhana balances the left and right sides of the brain, promoting mental clarity, reducing anxiety, and enhancing overall relaxation.
   * **4-7-8 Breathing:**
   * Inhale quietly through your nose for a count of four. Hold your breath for a count of seven. Exhale completely through your mouth for a count of eight. This completes one breath cycle. Repeat for several cycles.
   * 4-7-8 breathing is a calming technique that helps regulate the nervous system, inducing a sense of tranquility and easing stress.
   * **Resonant or Coherent Breathing:**
   * Inhale and exhale at a rate of about five breaths per minute, aiming for a smooth and even rhythm. Focus on making your inhalation and exhalation of equal duration.
   * Resonant breathing synchronizes heart rate variability, promoting coherence between the heart, respiratory system, and brain. This technique enhances relaxation and reduces stress.
   * **Sama Vritti (Equal Breathing):**
   * Inhale and exhale for an equal count. Start with a comfortable count, such as four, and gradually increase as you become more comfortable. Maintain the same duration for both inhalation and exhalation.
   * Sama Vritti calms the nervous system, improves focus, and provides a quick way to regain composure during stressful moments.

3. **4-7-8 Breathing (Relaxing Breath):**
   * Inhale quietly through your nose for a count of four, hold your breath for a count of seven, and exhale audibly through your mouth for a count of eight. Repeat the cycle for several breaths.
   * This technique is designed to induce a state of deep relaxation and is effective in managing anxiety and stress.

4. **Alternate Nostril Breathing (Nadi Shodhana):**
   * Sit comfortably with your spine straight.
     Close your right nostril with your right thumb and inhale deeply through your left nostril. Close your left nostril with your right ring finger, release your right nostril, and exhale. Inhale through the right nostril, close it, release the left nostril, and exhale. Repeat for several cycles.
   * Nadi Shodhana balances the flow of energy in the body, promoting mental clarity and relaxation.

5. **Ujjayi Breathing (Ocean Breath):**
   - Inhale slowly through your nose, slightly constricting the back of your throat to create a sound resembling ocean waves. Exhale with the same throat constriction. Focus on the sound and the sensation of breath. Repeat for several breaths.
   - Ujjayi breathing enhances concentration, reduces stress, and promotes a sense of inner calm.
6. **Resonant or Coherent Breathing:**
   - **Heart Rate Variability (HRV) Biofeedback:**
   - Use HRV biofeedback devices or apps to monitor and train coherent breathing. Follow visual or auditory cues to synchronize your breathing with your heart rate variability. Gradually adjust the pace to achieve a balanced and coherent physiological state.
   - HRV biofeedback enhances awareness of the body's responses to breathing, helping individuals refine their resonant breathing patterns for optimal stress reduction.
   - **Guided Resonant Breathing Meditations:**
   - Engage in guided meditation sessions that specifically focus on resonant or coherent breathing. Follow the voice or visual cues of a meditation guide to synchronize your breath with a harmonious rhythm.
   - Guided resonant breathing meditations provide structured support for individuals seeking to develop and maintain a coherent breathing practice, fostering relaxation and stress resilience.
   - **Progressive Resonance Breathing:**
   - Begin with a comfortable breathing rate, gradually increasing the duration of inhalation and exhalation. Aim for a smooth and even rhythm, allowing your breath to resonate through your body. Progressively extend the duration as you build familiarity.
   - Progressive resonance breathing involves a gradual and intentional progression toward longer breath cycles, promoting deeper relaxation and enhanced coherence in the autonomic nervous system.
   - **Mindful Resonant Breathing during Activities:**
   - Incorporate resonant breathing into daily activities. Whether walking, working, or engaging in routine tasks, maintain a resonant breathing rhythm. Pay attention to your breath as it resonates with the pace of your activities.
   - Mindful integration of resonant breathing into daily activities promotes sustained relaxation, reducing the cumulative impact of stressors throughout the day.
7. **Breath Counting:**
   - Inhale deeply and then exhale completely. Begin counting each inhalation and exhalation cycle, starting from one and going up to five. Once you reach five, restart the count. Focus on the breath and the counting.
   - Breath counting provides a simple yet effective way to anchor the mind, reduce distractions, and promote relaxation.
8. **Paced Breathing (Sama Vritti):**
   - Inhale for a specific count (e.g., four counts), hold the breath for the same count, exhale for the same count, and then pause before starting the next cycle.
   Paced breathing helps regulate the breath, induces a sense of calm, and can be easily adjusted to your preferred rhythm.
9. **Candle or Straw Breathing:**
   - Imagine you are blowing out a candle or trying to make a piece of paper move with your breath. Inhale deeply through your nose, and exhale slowly and steadily as if blowing through a straw.
   - This technique encourages slow and controlled exhalation, promoting relaxation and stress reduction.
10. **Sighing Breath:**
    - **Cleansing Sighs:**
    - Take several deep inhales through your nose, allowing your lungs to expand fully. Exhale with audible sighs, imagining you are releasing any accumulated stress or negativity. Repeat this process for several cycles.
    - Cleansing sighs provide a cathartic release, helping to clear the mind and body of tension, and promoting a sense of renewal.
    - **Mindful Sighing During Transitions:**
    - Integrate sighing breaths during transitions between activities or environments.

As you move from one task to another, take a moment to inhale deeply through your nose and exhale with a sigh. Use this practice to signal a mental shift and release any lingering stress.

- Mindful sighs during transitions serve as a mini-reset, helping to prevent the accumulation of stress throughout the day.
- **Group Sighing Exercise:**
- Gather a group of friends, family, or colleagues for a collective sighing exercise. Inhale together, and on the exhale, release a synchronized sigh. This shared experience can create a sense of connection and shared relaxation.
- Group sighing exercises foster a communal sense of stress relief, promoting a supportive and relaxed atmosphere.
- **Sighing Breath Visualization:**
- Close your eyes and visualize exhaling stress, worries, or tension with each sigh. Imagine the sigh carrying away any negative energy, leaving you feeling lighter and more at ease. Combining visualization with sighing breath amplifies the mental and emotional impact, enhancing the overall sense of relief.

11. **Bumblebee Breath (Bhramari Pranayama):**
    - Close your ears with your thumbs, place your index fingers on your forehead, and rest your remaining fingers on your closed eyes. Inhale deeply through your nose and exhale with a humming sound, like a bee.
      Repeat for several breaths.
    - Bhramari Pranayama helps calm the mind, reduce stress, and create a sense of inner peace.

12. **Mindful Breath Observation:**
    - **Anchor Points of Breath:**
    - Choose an anchor point for your breath observation, such as the sensation of air passing through your nostrils, the rise and fall of your chest, or the expansion and contraction of your diaphragm. Focus your attention on this chosen point.
    - Having a specific anchor point provides a stable focus for your breath observation, deepening your mindfulness practice and enhancing concentration.
    - **Body Scan with Breath Awareness:**
    - Combine mindful breath observation with a body scan. As you observe your breath, progressively bring awareness to different parts of your body, noting any sensations or tensions. This integrated practice enhances overall body-mind awareness.
    - The body scan fosters a holistic experience, promoting a deep connection between breath awareness and bodily sensations.
    - **Nature-Inspired Breath Observation:**
    - Practice breath observation in nature. Sit in a natural setting and observe your breath while immersing yourself in the sounds, scents, and sensations of the environment. Allow your breath to synchronize with the rhythm of nature.
    - Nature-inspired breath observation deepens the sense of presence and connection with the natural world, amplifying the calming effects of the practice.
    - **Breath Observation as a Grounding Technique:**
    - Use breath observation as a grounding technique during moments of anxiety or overwhelm.

Chapter 3

Body Awareness:
Learning from Your Own Signals

1. **Body Scan Meditation:**
   - **Customized Body Scan Meditation:**
   - Tailor your body scan meditation to focus on specific areas of tension or discomfort. Customize the practice based on your unique needs, allowing for a more targeted and personalized exploration.
   - A customized body scan enables you to address specific areas of concern, promoting targeted relaxation and stress relief.
   - **Mindful Breath Integration:**
   - Integrate mindful breathing into your body scan meditation. Coordinate your breath with the exploration of different body parts, syncing inhalations and exhalations with the awareness of sensations.
   - Combining breath awareness with the body scan enhances the mind-body connection, fostering a harmonious and calming experience.
   - **Body Scan for Pre-Sleep Relaxation:**
   - Use a body scan meditation as part of your pre-sleep routine. Starting from toes to head, systematically relax each body part. This practice promotes physical relaxation, easing the transition into a restful sleep.
   - Incorporating a body scan before bedtime encourages a sense of calmness, potentially improving sleep quality and reducing stress accumulated throughout the day.
   - **Dynamic Body Scan for Movement Awareness:**
   - Explore a dynamic body scan, incorporating gentle movements during the practice. Wiggle fingers, rotate ankles, or stretch limbs while maintaining awareness. This variation promotes not only stillness but also movement mindfulness.
   - Dynamic body scan adds an element of flexibility and movement awareness, making the practice adaptable to different preferences and promoting overall body-mind connection.
   - **Progressive Depth Body Scan:**
   - Progressively deepen your body scan by exploring sensations beyond the surface.
     Move from skin-deep awareness to muscles, bones, and internal organs. This layered approach enhances the depth of your mindfulness practice.
   - A progressive depth body scan provides a more comprehensive understanding of the intricacies within your body, fostering a profound sense of connection and awareness.
2. **Progressive Muscle Relaxation (PMR):**
   - Engage in progressive muscle relaxation, systematically tensing and then releasing different muscle groups. This technique helps you identify and release muscular tension, promoting overall physical relaxation.
   - PMR not only enhances body awareness but also serves as a practical tool for reducing physical stress and promoting a sense of calm.
3. **Intuitive Movement Practices:**
   - **Yoga Exploration:**
   - Engage in various styles of yoga, from gentle and restorative to more dynamic forms. Yoga postures, combined with conscious breathing, promote flexibility, strength, and heightened body awareness.
   - Yoga cultivates a mindful connection between breath and movement, fostering a sense of unity between mind and body. It enhances flexibility, balance, and overall physical well-being.
   - **Tai Chi Flow:**
   - Incorporate the flowing movements of Tai Chi into your routine. The deliberate and slow-paced sequences promote mindfulness, coordination, and a gentle connection with the body.
   - Tai Chi's rhythmic movements enhance body awareness, improve balance, and contribute to a sense of calm. It provides a meditative experience while promoting physical flexibility and grace.

- **Dance as Expression:**
- Engage in expressive dance, allowing your body to move freely to music. Whether structured or spontaneous, dance promotes self-expression, joy, and a profound awareness of your body's movements.
- Dance as an intuitive movement practice encourages a positive relationship with your body. It serves as a form of self-expression, promoting emotional release, and fostering a sense of liberation.
- **Walking Meditation:**
- Transform your daily walks into a mindful practice. Focus on each step, the sensation of your feet touching the ground, and your breath. Walking meditation integrates movement with mindfulness.
- Walking meditation offers a practical way to infuse mindfulness into everyday activities. It enhances awareness of body movements, promotes relaxation, and provides a mental break from daily stressors.

4. **Breath-Body Connection:**
   - Pay attention to how your breath relates to different emotions and physical sensations. Observe the breath during moments of stress, relaxation, and joy to understand its correlation with your emotional and physical state.
   - Recognizing the breath-body connection offers insights into the interplay between respiratory patterns, emotions, and stress, enabling proactive management of your well-being.

5. **Posture Awareness:**
   - Be mindful of your posture throughout the day.
     Notice how different postures impact your energy levels, mood, and stress levels. Make adjustments to promote comfortable and supportive body positions.
   - Maintaining awareness of your posture fosters a mindful approach to body mechanics, reducing the risk of physical discomfort and stress-related tension.

6. **Body Awareness Journaling:**
   - Keep a body awareness journal to track sensations, discomfort, or areas of tension. Note any patterns or correlations between your physical state and external factors such as work, relationships, or daily activities.
   - Journaling facilitates self-reflection, helping you uncover patterns in your body's responses to stressors and providing insights into areas that may need attention or care.

7. **Mindful Eating Practices:**
   - Practice mindful eating by paying attention to the sensory experience of each bite. Notice flavors, textures, and how your body responds to different foods. This fosters a connection between your nutritional choices and overall well-being.
   - Mindful eating cultivates body awareness, promoting a balanced approach to nourishment and reducing the potential for stress-related eating habits.

8. **Somatic Awareness Techniques:**
   - **Feldenkrais Method Exploration:**
   - Immerse yourself in the Feldenkrais Method, a somatic approach emphasizing awareness through gentle movements. Explore Feldenkrais lessons or classes to enhance your understanding of how your body moves and responds.
   - Feldenkrais fosters heightened sensitivity to subtle body sensations, promoting improved posture, flexibility, and overall movement coordination. It encourages a mindful exploration of body mechanics.
   - **Somatic Movement Classes:**
   - Attend somatic movement classes or workshops that integrate various somatic techniques. These classes may combine elements of Feldenkrais, Alexander Technique, and other approaches to offer a comprehensive somatic experience.
   - Somatic movement classes provide a structured environment for exploring different techniques.
     They enhance overall body awareness, promoting a holistic understanding of movement patterns and stress responses.

- **Mindful Body Scanning:**
- Apply somatic awareness principles to a focused body scan. Explore sensations, tensions, and movements in a methodical manner, incorporating principles from somatic practices for a more nuanced understanding.
- Mindful body scanning with a somatic approach deepens the connection between mind and body. It enhances awareness of subtle movements and tensions, contributing to a more comprehensive somatic experience.
- **Sensory Awareness Exercises:**
- Engage in sensory awareness exercises that focus on heightened perception of touch, sound, and movement. These exercises can be done individually or as part of somatic practices, emphasizing sensory exploration.
- Sensory awareness exercises enhance overall sensitivity to bodily signals, fostering a more profound connection with the present moment.
  They contribute to stress reduction by grounding the individual in their sensory experience.

9. **Tension Release Exercises (TRE):**
   - Incorporate tension release exercises into your routine. TRE involves simple exercises that induce a shaking or trembling response in the body, promoting the release of accumulated tension and stress.
   - TRE enhances body awareness by facilitating the discharge of stored tension, promoting physical and emotional well-being.

10. **Mindful Touch and Self-Massage:**
    - Engage in mindful touch or self-massage. Use your hands to explore areas of tension, applying gentle pressure and promoting relaxation. This practice encourages a tactile connection with your body.
    - Mindful touch and self-massage contribute to body awareness, providing a tangible way to address physical discomfort and stress-related tension.

11. **Temperature Sensation Awareness:**
    - Pay attention to temperature sensations in your body. Notice how warmth or coolness is experienced in different situations.
      This heightened awareness of temperature provides insights into your body's response to external conditions.
    - Temperature sensation awareness enhances your ability to create a comfortable environment, minimizing stressors related to thermal discomfort.

12. **Interceptive Awareness:**
    - Cultivate interceptive awareness by tuning into internal bodily signals, such as heartbeat, breathing, or digestive sensations. This practice deepens your understanding of the physiological aspects of stress.
    - Interceptive awareness connects you to your body's internal processes, offering valuable information about your emotional and physical state, and aiding in stress regulation.

13. **Grounding Techniques:**
    - Practice grounding techniques, such as placing your feet on the ground, to foster a sense of connection with the Earth. Pay attention to the sensations in your feet and legs, promoting a feeling of stability and support.
    - Grounding techniques enhance body awareness by bringing attention to the present moment, reducing the impact of stressors on your overall well-being.

Chapter 4

Observing Without Judgment:
A Key to Inner Peace

- **Mindful Awareness Practices:**
  - **Body Scan Meditation:**
  - Incorporate body scan meditation into your mindfulness routine. Systematically bring attention to each part of your body, observing sensations without judgment. This practice enhances your ability to be present in the body without assigning positive or negative labels.
  - Body scan meditation deepens the connection between mind and body. By observing physical sensations without judgment, you cultivate a heightened awareness of your body's signals and contribute to a more peaceful internal state.
  - **Walking Meditation:**
  - Integrate walking meditation into your routine. Focus on each step, the sensations in your feet, and the movement of your body. Notice thoughts and let them pass without judgment as you continue walking mindfully.
  - Walking meditation adds a dynamic element to mindfulness. It encourages observing without judgment in motion, fostering a sense of presence and tranquility. This practice can be particularly beneficial for those who find sitting meditation challenging.
  - **Loving-Kindness Meditation:**
  - Explore loving-kindness meditation, directing compassionate thoughts towards yourself and others. Observe any resistance or judgments that arise during the practice, allowing them to be without attaching further evaluation.
  - Loving-kindness meditation promotes a kind and open-hearted approach to oneself and others. By observing judgments without getting entangled in them, this practice contributes to a more compassionate and harmonious mindset.
- **Cultivating a Witness Mindset:**
  - Cultivate a "witness mindset" by consciously stepping back from your thoughts and emotions. Imagine yourself as an impartial observer, acknowledging the flow of experiences without becoming entangled in them.
  - Developing a witness mindset allows you to detach from the constant stream of thoughts and emotions. It promotes a sense of inner calm by creating distance between yourself and the ever-changing nature of your internal landscape.
- **Non-Identification with Thoughts:**
  - **Mindful Labeling:**
  - Incorporate mindful labeling into your non-identification practice. When a thought arises, label it without judgment as a "thought" or "thinking." This simple act helps create distance between yourself and the thought, reducing the tendency to fuse with it.
  - Mindful labeling enhances the objectivity of observing thoughts. It reinforces the idea that thoughts are mental events, not absolute truths. This practice contributes to a more detached and non-identifying relationship with the thought process.
  - **Thought Cloud Visualization:**
  - Imagine your thoughts as clouds passing through the sky. Visualize each thought as a distinct cloud, drifting by without lingering. Observe the thoughts with curiosity but without attaching personal significance to any specific cloud.
  - Thought cloud visualization provides a metaphorical representation of the transient nature of thoughts. It fosters a sense of impermanence, aiding in the non-identification process by portraying thoughts as passing phenomena.
  - **Thought Diary:**
  - Keep a thought diary where you jot down recurring or challenging thoughts without judgment. Note the emotions associated with each thought. Regularly reviewing the diary can provide insights into thought patterns and reinforce the practice of non-identification.

- A thought diary serves as an objective record of thoughts. It helps identify patterns and triggers without getting entangled in the emotional content. This practice enhances self-awareness and supports the non-identification process.
  - **Thoughts as Passing Trains:**
  - Picture your thoughts as trains arriving at and departing from a train station. Each thought represents a train, and you are the observer on the platform. Watch the thoughts come and go without boarding any particular train.
  - The train metaphor reinforces the transitory nature of thoughts. By choosing not to board any specific train (thought), you cultivate a non-identifying stance, recognizing that thoughts are passing events within the mind.
- **Acceptance and Commitment Therapy (ACT):**
  - Explore ACT principles, emphasizing acceptance of thoughts and feelings rather than judgment. Acknowledge and make room for uncomfortable thoughts and emotions, allowing them to exist without resistance.
  - ACT promotes psychological flexibility by encouraging acceptance of the present moment. By accepting thoughts without judgment, inner peace is cultivated through a more harmonious relationship with the complexities of the mind.
- **Compassionate Self-Observation:**
  - Approach self-observation with compassion. When noticing thoughts or behaviors, instead of criticizing, respond with understanding and kindness. Cultivate a nurturing inner dialogue that encourages growth and self-compassion.

  - Compassionate self-observation fosters a positive and supportive relationship with oneself. It diminishes the harsh inner critic, creating space for self-acceptance and contributing to a more peaceful internal environment.
- **Mindful Journaling:**
  - Keep a mindful journal to document thoughts and feelings without judgment. Write down observations of experiences, allowing the act of writing to create a separation between you and the observed content.
  - Mindful journaling serves as a tool for self-reflection without the burden of judgment. It provides a safe space to explore thoughts and emotions, fostering a sense of clarity and understanding.
- **Mindful Eating Practices:**
  - **Sensory Exploration:**
  - Engage in sensory exploration during meals. Observe the aroma, texture, and temperature of your food. Allow each bite to be a unique sensory experience without immediately categorizing it as pleasurable or displeasurable.
  - Sensory exploration enhances the richness of the eating experience. By observing without judgment, you cultivate a more present and mindful approach to meals, fostering a deeper connection with the act of eating.
  - **Mindful Portion Control:**
  - Practice mindful portion control by serving reasonable amounts of food. Avoid judgmental thoughts about portion sizes and listen to your body's signals of hunger and fullness. Allow yourself to eat in a way that honors your body's needs without attaching guilt or praise.
  - Mindful portion control promotes a balanced relationship with food. By observing without judgment, you create an environment where eating is guided by body signals rather than external judgments, contributing to a healthier and more intuitive approach to nourishment.
  - **Non-Judgmental Reflections:**
  - After a meal, reflect on the experience without judgment. Notice any thoughts or feelings that arise, such as satisfaction or potential self-criticism. Approach these reflections with curiosity and acceptance, allowing them to be without attaching moral value.
  - Non-judgmental reflections support self-awareness. By observing post-meal thoughts without criticism, you foster a more compassionate understanding of your relationship with food, contributing to improved emotional well-being.

- **Gratitude for Nourishment:**
  - Express gratitude for the nourishment your meal provides. Cultivate an appreciation for the effort that went into preparing the food and the nutrients it offers your body. Approach the act of eating with a sense of gratitude without evaluating the meal's worth.
  - Gratitude for nourishment shifts the focus from judgment to appreciation. By acknowledging the positive aspects of the eating experience, you create a more positive and balanced mindset around food, supporting overall well-being.
- **Focused Attention Meditation:**
  - Incorporate focused attention meditation, directing your awareness to a specific object, sound, or sensation. When distractions arise, return to your focal point without criticizing yourself. Cultivate a gentle redirection of attention.
  - Focused attention meditation hones the skill of observing without judgment. It strengthens your capacity to remain present and centered, fostering a calm and undisturbed state of mind.
- **Mindfulness in Everyday Activities:**
  - Extend mindfulness to daily activities such as walking, washing dishes, or commuting. Engage in these activities with full attention, observing the sensations, movements, and surroundings without evaluating them.
  - Infusing mindfulness into everyday activities enhances your ability to observe without judgment. It transforms routine tasks into opportunities for presence, contributing to a more peaceful and centered state of being.
- **Reflective Pause in Decision-Making:**
  - Before making decisions, take a reflective pause. Observe your thoughts and emotions without immediately reacting. Create space for clarity and discernment, allowing choices to emerge from a place of calm observation.
  - A reflective pause minimizes impulsive reactions driven by judgment. It promotes thoughtful decision-making, reducing stress and fostering a sense of inner peace through intentional choices.
- **Mindful Communication:**
  - Practice mindful communication by listening actively and responding with awareness. Observe your own words and thoughts without immediate judgment, fostering a non-reactive and empathetic communication style.
  - Mindful communication contributes to a peaceful interpersonal environment. It allows for a more understanding and compassionate exchange of ideas, reducing potential conflicts and promoting harmonious relationships.
- **Nature Observation Meditation:**
  - Spend time in nature, observing the environment without judgment. Practice nature meditation by focusing on the sights, sounds, and sensations around you. Allow nature to be a source of inspiration and a reminder of non-judgmental observation.
  - Nature observation meditation connects you to the present moment and the beauty of the natural world.

Part Four:
Emotional Resilience

Chapter 1

Building
Emotional Strength

1. **Emotional Awareness:**
   - **Mindful Expression of Emotions:**
   - Engage in mindful expression of emotions. Instead of suppressing or avoiding emotions, find healthy outlets for their expression. This could include talking to a trusted friend, journaling, or engaging in creative activities like art or music.
   - Mindful expression fosters emotional release and understanding. By allowing emotions to flow in a controlled and mindful manner, you prevent the build-up of emotional tension, contributing to emotional resilience.
   - **Emotional Regulation Techniques:**
   - Learn and practice emotional regulation techniques such as deep breathing, progressive muscle relaxation, or guided imagery. These techniques help you manage intense emotions in the moment, promoting a sense of control and stability.
   - Emotional regulation techniques provide practical tools for navigating challenging emotional experiences.
   By incorporating these techniques into your routine, you enhance your capacity to respond to stressors with composure and resilience.
   - **Cultivating Empathy:**
   - Cultivate empathy by putting yourself in others' shoes. Seek to understand different perspectives and emotions, both in yourself and those around you. This practice develops emotional intelligence and promotes more compassionate responses to challenging situations.
   - Cultivating empathy strengthens interpersonal relationships and fosters a sense of connection. By understanding the emotions of others, you contribute to a supportive and empathetic social environment, enhancing overall emotional well-being.
2. **Mindful Acceptance:**
   - Practice mindful acceptance of your emotions without judgment. Allow yourself to experience feelings without labeling them as good or bad. Mindful breathing or meditation can aid in creating a non-reactive space for emotions.
   - Mindful acceptance fosters resilience. By acknowledging and accepting emotions, even uncomfortable ones, you build the capacity to navigate challenging situations with greater ease.
3. **Cultivating Positive Emotions:**
   - Actively cultivate positive emotions by engaging in activities that bring joy, gratitude, or satisfaction. This could include spending time with loved ones, pursuing hobbies, or practicing gratitude.
   - Building a reservoir of positive emotions enhances emotional strength. Positivity acts as a buffer during stressful times, contributing to overall emotional well-being.
4. **Emotional Regulation:**
   - Learn and practice emotional regulation techniques. This may involve deep-breathing exercises, progressive muscle relaxation, or guided imagery to calm the nervous system during emotionally charged moments.
   - Emotional regulation prevents emotional overwhelm. By having tools to manage intense feelings, you empower yourself to respond to stressors with greater composure.
5. **Resilient Thinking Patterns:**
   - **Cognitive Flexibility:**
   - Cultivate cognitive flexibility by being open to alternative perspectives and solutions. Challenge rigid thinking and explore different angles when faced with challenges. Embrace adaptability in your thought processes.
   - Cognitive flexibility enhances resilience by fostering a more adaptable and versatile mindset. By considering multiple viewpoints, you broaden your approach to problem-solving, contributing to emotional strength.

- **Affirmation of Personal Strengths:**
- Affirm your personal strengths and capabilities regularly. Acknowledge your past achievements and successes. This practice reinforces a positive self-image and empowers you to face challenges with confidence.
- Affirming personal strengths builds a foundation for resilience. By recognizing your abilities and accomplishments, you cultivate a sense of self-efficacy, which serves as a source of emotional strength during challenging times.
- **Learned Optimism:**
- Foster learned optimism by cultivating a positive explanatory style. When facing setbacks, attribute them to external, temporary, and specific factors rather than internal, permanent, and pervasive ones. Practice reframing negative events with a focus on optimistic explanations.
- Learned optimism contributes to emotional resilience. By adopting a positive explanatory style, you build a mindset that views setbacks as temporary and surmountable, reducing the impact of stress on your emotional well-being.

6. **Healthy Coping Mechanisms:**
   - Identify and adopt healthy coping mechanisms for stress. This might include talking to a friend, engaging in creative outlets, or practicing relaxation techniques.
   - Healthy coping mechanisms contribute to emotional strength by providing constructive outlets for stress. Avoiding maladaptive coping strategies helps maintain emotional well-being.

7. **Building a Support System:**
   - Cultivate a strong support system by fostering meaningful connections with friends, family, or support groups. Share your thoughts and feelings with trusted individuals who offer understanding and encouragement.
   - A robust support system bolsters emotional strength. Knowing you have a network to lean on during challenging times provides a sense of security and resilience.

8. **Setting Boundaries:**
   - Establish and maintain healthy boundaries in personal and professional relationships. Clearly communicate your limits, and prioritize self-care to prevent emotional exhaustion.
   - Setting boundaries is vital for emotional strength. It ensures that you allocate time and energy in a way that aligns with your well-being, preventing burnout and emotional depletion.

9. **Mindfulness-Based Cognitive Therapy (MBCT):**
   - Engage in MBCT, a therapeutic approach combining mindfulness meditation with cognitive-behavioral therapy principles.
     It's designed to prevent the recurrence of depressive episodes and build emotional resilience.
   - MBCT enhances emotional strength by promoting a balanced and non-reactive awareness of thoughts and emotions. It equips individuals with tools to navigate emotional challenges skillfully.

10. **Embracing Vulnerability:**
    - **Expressing Emotions Authentically:**
    - Allow yourself to express a range of emotions authentically. Avoid suppressing or denying feelings, whether they are positive or negative. Share your emotions with trusted individuals or through creative outlets.
    - Expressing emotions authentically enhances emotional strength. By acknowledging and expressing your feelings, you cultivate a healthy relationship with your emotional experiences, fostering resilience in the face of challenges.
    - **Building Supportive Relationships:**
    - Build and nurture relationships that provide emotional support. Surround yourself with individuals who accept you for who you are and encourage open communication.
    - Building supportive relationships is a key aspect of embracing vulnerability. By connecting with others in an authentic way, you create a network of support that contributes to emotional resilience and a sense of belonging.
    - **Seeking Professional Guidance:**
    - If needed, seek professional guidance from therapists or counselors. Professional support offers a confidential space to explore and address vulnerabilities. Therapeutic interventions can provide tools to cope with challenges and enhance emotional well-being.

- Seeking professional guidance is a proactive step in embracing vulnerability. By working with a mental health professional, you gain insights, coping strategies, and a supportive environment for addressing vulnerabilities and building emotional strength.

11. **Mindful Self-Compassion:**
- Practice mindful self-compassion by treating yourself with kindness during difficult times. Acknowledge your struggles without self-judgment, fostering a supportive internal dialogue.
- Mindful self-compassion builds emotional strength by promoting a positive and nurturing relationship with oneself. It acts as a buffer against the negative impact of self-criticism and perfectionism.

12. **Reflective Practices:**
- Engage in reflective practices, such as journaling or meditation, to explore deeper emotions and gain insights into your inner world. Reflective practices foster self-awareness and emotional growth.
- Reflective practices contribute to emotional strength by providing a space for self-discovery and understanding. They facilitate personal growth and resilience in the face of life's challenges.

13. **Gratitude Practices:**
- Cultivate gratitude as a daily practice. Acknowledge and express gratitude for positive aspects of your life. This intentional focus on gratitude enhances emotional strength by shifting the focus from what's lacking to what's present.
- Gratitude practices contribute to emotional strength by fostering a positive mindset and reducing the impact of negativity. They promote a resilient and appreciative outlook on life.

14. **Therapeutic Support:**
- Seek therapeutic support when needed. A mental health professional can provide guidance, tools, and a safe space to explore and strengthen emotional resilience.
- Therapeutic support is invaluable for building emotional strength. It offers tailored strategies and insights to address specific emotional challenges, fostering long-term well-being.

Chapter 2

Cultivating Positivity
and Gratitude

1. **Gratitude Journaling:**
   - Maintain a gratitude journal where you regularly jot down things you are thankful for. Reflect on positive experiences, acts of kindness, or moments of joy. This practice directs your focus toward positive aspects of your life.
   - Gratitude journaling cultivates positivity by fostering a habit of acknowledging and appreciating the good in your life. It shifts your mindset from dwelling on stressors to actively recognizing and savoring positive elements.
2. **Three Good Things Exercise:**
   - Each day, identify three positive things that happened. These could be small accomplishments, moments of joy, or acts of kindness from others. Reflect on why each of these events was meaningful to you.
   - The Three Good Things exercise reinforces positivity by encouraging daily reflection on positive experiences. It helps train your mind to notice and appreciate the positive aspects of your life, contributing to an optimistic outlook.
3. **Positive Affirmations:**
   - **Gratitude Practices Beyond Journaling:**
   - Expand your gratitude practices beyond journaling. Express gratitude directly to people in your life, either through verbal communication, handwritten notes, or thoughtful gestures. Actively acknowledge and appreciate the positive contributions of others.
   - Directly expressing gratitude fosters positivity in relationships and amplifies the impact of your gratitude. By verbalizing your appreciation, you contribute to a positive and uplifting environment, enhancing overall well-being.
   - **Acts of Kindness:**
   - Engage in acts of kindness towards others without expecting anything in return. Random acts of kindness, whether small or significant, contribute to a positive mindset and cultivate a sense of purpose and connection.
   - Acts of kindness generate positive emotions and contribute to a more positive worldview. By actively participating in kindness, you not only brighten someone else's day but also enhance your own sense of fulfillment and positivity.
   - **Visualization of Positive Outcomes:**
   - Use visualization techniques to imagine positive outcomes and experiences. Create mental images of achieving your goals, experiencing joy, or overcoming challenges. Visualization helps reinforce positive expectations and beliefs.
   - Visualization enhances positivity by programming your mind to anticipate positive outcomes. By regularly visualizing success and positive scenarios, you cultivate a more optimistic mindset, contributing to resilience in the face of challenges.
   - **Positive Media Consumption:**
   - Consciously choose positive and uplifting media content. Whether it's books, movies, music, or online content, opt for material that inspires, motivates, and brings joy. Limit exposure to negative or distressing media that can contribute to stress.
   - Positive media consumption contributes to a more optimistic outlook. By surrounding yourself with uplifting content, you create an environment that supports a positive mindset and reinforces gratitude and positivity.
4. **Acts of Kindness:**
   - Engage in acts of kindness toward others without expecting anything in return. Acts of kindness could be as simple as helping a colleague, expressing gratitude, or supporting a friend. These actions contribute to a positive and compassionate mindset.

- Acts of kindness promote positivity by creating a sense of connection and purpose. By focusing on helping others, you enhance your own well-being and contribute to a more positive and supportive social environment.

5. **Savoring Positive Experiences:**
   - Practice savoring positive experiences by fully engaging in and appreciating enjoyable moments. Whether it's a delicious meal, a beautiful sunset, or a personal achievement, take the time to savor and relish these positive moments.
   - Savoring positive experiences enhances positivity by increasing your awareness and appreciation of joyful moments. It contributes to a more mindful and optimistic approach to daily life.

6. **Positive Visualization:**
   - Engage in positive visualization by imagining successful outcomes and positive scenarios. Visualize yourself overcoming challenges, achieving goals, and experiencing moments of happiness. This mental rehearsal fosters a positive mindset.
   - Positive visualization cultivates positivity by programming your mind to focus on favorable outcomes. It helps build confidence, resilience, and a positive expectation for the future.

7. **Gratitude Practices in Relationships:**
   - Express gratitude within your relationships. Regularly acknowledge and appreciate the qualities, actions, and support provided by friends, family, and colleagues. Share your gratitude verbally or through written notes.
   - Gratitude practices in relationships strengthen connections and contribute to a positive social environment. By expressing and receiving gratitude, you foster a supportive and uplifting atmosphere in your personal and professional relationships.

8. **Positive Media Consumption:**
   - Consciously choose positive and uplifting media content.
     Limit exposure to negative news or content that induces stress. Select books, movies, and online content that inspire, motivate, and contribute to a positive mindset.
   - Positive media consumption influences your mindset by shaping your thoughts and emotions. By surrounding yourself with uplifting content, you create an environment that nurtures positivity and reduces the impact of external stressors.

9. **Mindful Positivity in Conversations:**
   - Be mindful of your language and tone in conversations. Aim to infuse positivity into your communication by using encouraging words, expressing optimism, and highlighting solutions. Foster a positive atmosphere in your interactions.
   - Mindful positivity in conversations contributes to a more uplifting social environment. By choosing positive language and framing discussions in an optimistic manner, you enhance the overall positivity of your relationships and interactions.

10. **Reflecting on Personal Growth:**
    - Regularly reflect on your personal growth and accomplishments.
      Celebrate achievements, both big and small. Acknowledge the progress you've made in various aspects of your life, fostering a positive sense of self.
    - Reflecting on personal growth cultivates positivity by recognizing and appreciating your journey. By acknowledging your efforts and achievements, you reinforce a positive self-image and build confidence in your ability to overcome challenges.

11. **Positive Focus in Problem-Solving:**
    - Approach problem-solving with a positive focus. Instead of dwelling on obstacles, actively seek solutions and opportunities for growth. Frame challenges as learning experiences and focus on constructive actions.
    - A positive focus in problem-solving enhances resilience by shifting your mindset from a problem-oriented to a solution-oriented approach. It encourages proactive and optimistic responses to challenges.

12. **Creating a Positivity Jar:**
    - Maintain a positivity jar where you place notes about positive experiences, achievements, or moments of gratitude. Whenever you need a boost, revisit these notes to remind yourself of the positive aspects of your life.

- Creating a positivity jar reinforces positivity by providing a tangible reminder of the good in your life. It serves as a visual representation of positive experiences, contributing to an optimistic mindset.

13. **Gratitude Walks:**
    - Incorporate gratitude into your walks by reflecting on things you're grateful for while enjoying nature. Focus on the beauty around you, the sensations of walking, and the positive aspects of your life.
    - Gratitude walks combine physical activity with mindfulness, enhancing your overall well-being. By connecting with nature and expressing gratitude during walks, you foster a positive and rejuvenating experience.

14. **Celebrating Small Wins:**
    - **Reflection on Personal Growth:**
    - Regularly reflect on your personal growth and development. Acknowledge the progress you've made in various aspects of your life, whether it's acquiring new skills, overcoming fears, or enhancing self-awareness.
    - Reflecting on personal growth reinforces a positive self-image. By recognizing and appreciating the journey of self-improvement, you cultivate a sense of achievement and optimism about your capabilities.
    - **Expressing Gratitude for Challenges:**
    - Develop the habit of expressing gratitude for challenges and setbacks. Instead of viewing difficulties as purely negative, consider them as opportunities for learning and growth. Express gratitude for the lessons they bring.
    - Expressing gratitude for challenges reframes your perspective. By embracing challenges as valuable experiences, you cultivate resilience and a positive outlook on the opportunities for learning and development they provide.
    - **Positive Visualization for Future Success:**
    - Engage in positive visualization for future success. Create mental images of achieving your goals and experiencing fulfillment in various aspects of your life. Visualize the positive outcomes you aspire to achieve.
    - Positive visualization for future success fuels motivation.
      By vividly imagining the achievement of your goals, you instill confidence and enthusiasm, contributing to a positive mindset and determination.
    - **Gratitude for Support Systems:**
    - Express gratitude for the support systems in your life. Acknowledge and appreciate the individuals who provide encouragement, guidance, and companionship. Regularly communicate your gratitude to strengthen these positive connections.
    - Gratitude for support systems enhances positive relationships. By recognizing and thanking those who contribute positively to your life, you nurture a supportive network that fosters positivity and emotional well-being.

15. **Morning Positivity Rituals:**
    - Start your day with positivity rituals, such as morning affirmations, gratitude reflections, or visualization of a positive day ahead. Set a positive tone for the day by incorporating these rituals into your morning routine.
    - Morning positivity rituals influence your mindset for the day, contributing to a more optimistic and resilient approach.

Chapter 3

The Role of Vulnerability
in Stress Management

- **Understanding Vulnerability:**
  - **Developing Resilience through Vulnerability:**
  - Recognize vulnerability as a pathway to building resilience. When you face challenges with an open and authentic attitude, it becomes an opportunity to develop resilience – the ability to bounce back from adversity.
  - Embracing vulnerability cultivates adaptability, enabling you to navigate unforeseen stressors with greater flexibility and a positive mindset.
  - **Vulnerability as a Source of Growth:**
  - Understand that vulnerability is intricately linked to personal growth. When you step into situations with vulnerability, you expose yourself to new experiences, learning opportunities, and personal development.
  - Embracing vulnerability involves stepping outside of your comfort zone, and it is in these moments of discomfort that substantial personal growth often occurs.
  - **Connecting Vulnerability and Authenticity:**
  - Acknowledge that vulnerability and authenticity are closely intertwined. Authentic living involves embracing and expressing vulnerability, allowing you to live in alignment with your true self.
  - By being vulnerable, you reduce the need for pretense or putting on a facade, leading to more genuine and fulfilling connections with yourself and others.
  - **Vulnerability in Decision-Making:**
  - Incorporate vulnerability into your decision-making process. Acknowledge that decisions come with uncertainties, and being vulnerable to the potential outcomes allows for more informed and mindful choices.
  - Embracing vulnerability in decision-making can alleviate stress by embracing the reality that not all decisions will have predictable outcomes.
  - **Cultivating Emotional Agility:**
  - Vulnerability involves accepting and navigating a range of emotions. Cultivate emotional agility by acknowledging and working through complex emotions, which contributes to overall emotional well-being.
- **Vulnerability as Strength:**
  - Recognize vulnerability as a source of strength rather than weakness. Embracing vulnerability means acknowledging and owning your authentic self, which fosters resilience in the face of stressors.
  - Viewing vulnerability as strength reframes stressors as opportunities for growth and self-discovery rather than threats.
- **Authentic Expression of Emotions:**
  - Allow yourself to authentically express emotions, including those traditionally seen as signs of vulnerability such as fear, sadness, or uncertainty. Suppressing emotions can contribute to stress, while authentic expression promotes emotional well-being.
  - By embracing and expressing vulnerability through emotions, you create a healthier emotional landscape, reducing the emotional burden that often accompanies stress.
- **Vulnerability in Relationships:**
  - **Reciprocity of Vulnerability:**
  - Encourage reciprocal vulnerability within relationships.
    When both parties feel safe to share their thoughts, fears, and aspirations, it creates a balanced exchange that deepens the connection.
  - Mutual vulnerability builds intimacy, fostering a deeper understanding of each other. This emotional closeness becomes a source of comfort and resilience during stressful periods.
  - **Navigating Conflict with Vulnerability:**

- Use vulnerability as a tool for open communication during conflicts. Sharing vulnerabilities allows for a more empathetic and constructive discussion, reducing tension and facilitating conflict resolution.
- Embracing vulnerability in conflicts helps develop effective conflict resolution skills, creating an environment where differences are acknowledged and addressed with respect.
- **Setting Boundaries through Vulnerability:**
- Communicate boundaries with vulnerability. When setting boundaries, express your needs and limitations openly, allowing for a clear understanding between individuals.
- Embracing vulnerability in boundary-setting fosters mutual respect, ensuring that each person's limits are acknowledged and honored. This contributes to a healthier and less stressful relationship dynamic.
- **Cultivating Trust through Vulnerability:**
- Practice transparency as a form of vulnerability. Sharing your authentic self, including fears and uncertainties, builds a foundation of trust within relationships.
- Embracing vulnerability reduces mistrust by demonstrating authenticity. When individuals feel secure in being themselves, it fosters a positive and trusting relationship environment.

- **Setting Boundaries and Saying No:**
  - Embrace vulnerability by setting and communicating boundaries. Acknowledge your limitations and be willing to say no when necessary to protect your well-being. This practice prevents burnout and overwhelm.
  - Vulnerability in setting boundaries reduces the likelihood of being overwhelmed by commitments, contributing to a more balanced and stress-resilient life.
- **Learning from Mistakes:**
  - View mistakes and failures as opportunities for growth rather than as personal shortcomings. Embrace vulnerability by recognizing that making mistakes is a natural part of the human experience.
  - Shifting the perspective on mistakes reduces the fear of failure, making it easier to navigate challenges without excessive stress. Vulnerability in learning contributes to adaptability and resilience.
- **Self-Compassion as Vulnerability:**
  - Embrace vulnerability by practicing self-compassion during difficult times. Treat yourself with kindness and understanding, recognizing that everyone faces challenges and setbacks.
  - Self-compassion in vulnerability alleviates self-criticism and judgment, reducing the emotional toll of stress. It fosters a supportive internal dialogue during challenging moments.
- **Balancing Control and Surrender:**
  - Embrace vulnerability by finding a balance between maintaining control and surrendering to the uncertainties of life.
  Accept that not everything can be controlled, and vulnerability lies in navigating the unknown.
  - Balancing control and surrender reduces the anxiety associated with the need for control. Embracing vulnerability in uncertainty contributes to a more adaptive and less stress-inducing mindset.
- **Vulnerability in Goal Setting:**
  - **Embracing Failure as a Learning Opportunity:**
  - Embrace vulnerability by reframing setbacks as opportunities for learning and growth. Rather than viewing failure as a negative outcome, recognize it as a natural part of the goal-setting process.
  - When setbacks occur, extract valuable lessons from the experience. Vulnerability in acknowledging failures allows for a deeper understanding of oneself and the factors influencing goal attainment.
  - **Seeking Support and Guidance:**
  - Embrace vulnerability by expressing your needs for support and guidance. Whether seeking advice from mentors, coaches, or peers, acknowledging that you can't achieve goals in isolation contributes to a healthier goal-setting approach.
  - Establish a support system that understands and respects your vulnerabilities. Sharing your goals with others creates accountability and provides a network to lean on during challenging moments.

- **Adjusting Goals Flexibly:**
- Acknowledge vulnerability by being flexible in adjusting goals as circumstances change. Life is dynamic, and adapting goals with vulnerability in mind allows for a more resilient response to unexpected challenges.
- Developing adaptability in goal setting reduces the stress associated with rigid expectations. Embracing vulnerability enables a more fluid and responsive approach to achieving desired outcomes.
- **Celebrating Progress, Not Just End Results:**
- Embrace vulnerability by celebrating progress, not just the final achievement. Acknowledge and celebrate small milestones along the way, fostering a positive mindset and reducing the pressure associated with achieving the ultimate goal.
- Celebrating progress builds confidence and resilience. By recognizing the steps taken, individuals cultivate a sense of accomplishment that contributes to overall well-being.
- **Mindful Vulnerability Practices:**
  - Incorporate mindfulness into vulnerability practices by mindfully reflecting on experiences, emotions, and reactions. Mindful vulnerability involves non-judgmental awareness and acceptance of the present moment.
  - Mindful vulnerability practices enhance stress management by cultivating a present-moment awareness that allows for a more measured and intentional response to stressors.
- **Vulnerability in Seeking Support:**
  - **Flexibility in Goal Adjustment:**
  - Embrace vulnerability by being open to adjusting goals based on changing circumstances. Acknowledge that unexpected challenges may arise, and flexibility in goal setting allows for a more adaptive response.
  - Viewing setbacks as opportunities for growth fosters a resilient mindset. Vulnerability in goal setting involves learning from challenges and adjusting strategies without self-judgment.
  - **Sharing Goals with Others:**
  - Embrace vulnerability by sharing your goals with trusted individuals.
    Building accountability within a supportive network creates a sense of shared responsibility, motivating progress and reducing the stress of solo endeavors.
  - Sharing goals allows for the reception of encouragement and support, contributing to a positive and affirming environment. This collective support enhances motivation and resilience.
  - **Vulnerability and Intrinsic Motivation:**
  - Acknowledge vulnerability by aligning goals with personal values. Connecting goals to intrinsic motivations creates a deeper sense of purpose and fulfillment, reducing the external pressures that can contribute to stress.
  - Intrinsic motivation involves embracing imperfections in the pursuit of goals. Vulnerability in goal setting includes acknowledging that the journey may not be flawless and that learning from imperfections is part of the process.

Chapter 4

Accepting and Letting Go

1. **Mindfulness-Based Acceptance:**
   - **Acceptance of Unpleasant Emotions:**
   - Practice acknowledging and accepting even the unpleasant or uncomfortable emotions that arise. Instead of resisting or suppressing them, allow yourself to observe these emotions with compassion and without judgment.
   - **Grounding Techniques:**
   - Combine mindfulness with grounding techniques to anchor yourself in the present. Techniques like grounding exercises involving the senses (sight, touch, smell) can enhance the experience of acceptance by connecting you with the immediate environment.
   - **Mindful Observation of Thoughts:**
   - Extend mindfulness to observe your thoughts as passing events. Recognize that thoughts, whether positive or negative, come and go. Cultivate a non-attachment to the content of thoughts, fostering a mindset of acceptance.
   - **Non-Attachment to Outcomes:**
   - Apply mindfulness to detach from rigid attachment to specific outcomes. Instead of fixating on a particular result, focus on the process and appreciate the journey. Non-attachment reduces the distress associated with unrealized expectations.
   - **Compassionate Self-Reflection:**
   - Use mindfulness as a tool for compassionate self-reflection. When faced with challenges or mistakes, approach self-reflection with kindness rather than harsh self-judgment. This practice supports self-acceptance and personal growth.
   - **Present-Moment Awareness in Daily Activities:**
   - Extend mindfulness beyond formal meditation sessions by incorporating present-moment awareness into daily activities. Whether it's eating, walking, or engaging in routine tasks, approach each moment with intentional attention and acceptance.
2. **Radical Acceptance:**
   - Practice radical acceptance by acknowledging and fully embracing the reality of a situation without judgment.
   This technique involves letting go of the struggle against what cannot be changed and finding peace in acceptance.
3. **Understanding Impermanence:**
   - Develop an understanding of impermanence, recognizing that situations, emotions, and experiences are constantly changing. Embracing impermanence helps in letting go of attachments to specific outcomes or circumstances.
4. **Mindful Breathing for Release:**
   - Use mindful breathing techniques as a tool for letting go. Inhale deeply, consciously holding onto tension, and exhale, visualizing the release of that tension. This practice fosters a sense of calm and encourages letting go of stress.
5. **The Art of Surrender:**
   - **Letting Go of Control Illusion:**
   - Reflect on the illusion of control. Acknowledge that there are aspects of life beyond your control, and surrender involves releasing the need to micromanage every detail.
   - **Mindful Release Rituals:**
   - Create mindful release rituals to symbolize surrender. This could include writing down worries on paper and then ceremoniously letting them go, signifying a conscious release of burdens.
   - **Yielding to the Flow of Life:**
   - Embrace the analogy of life as a river. Surrender involves yielding to the natural flow rather than resisting the current. Trust that, like a river, life will unfold in its own way.
   - **Acceptance of Uncertainty:**

- Practice accepting uncertainty. Surrendering to the unknown aspects of life involves acknowledging that not everything can be predicted or controlled.
- **Faith or Trust-Based Surrender:**
- For those with a spiritual inclination, surrender can involve placing trust in a higher power or the universe. This faith-based surrender allows individuals to relinquish control and find solace in divine guidance.
- **Embracing Change as a Constant:**
- Surrender to the inevitability of change.
  Recognize that life is dynamic, and surrendering involves embracing change without unnecessary resistance.

6. **Thought Defusion Techniques:**
   - Utilize thought defusion techniques to distance yourself from distressing thoughts. Rather than being entangled in negative thinking, observe thoughts as passing events, making it easier to let go of unhelpful patterns.

7. **Forgiveness Practices:**
   - Engage in forgiveness practices, both for yourself and others. Forgiveness is a powerful tool for letting go of resentment and negative emotions. It involves releasing the emotional burden associated with past experiences.

8. **Cultivating Gratitude:**
   - Cultivate gratitude as a way of shifting focus from what is lacking to what is present. Regularly acknowledge and appreciate the positive aspects of your life. Gratitude practices contribute to a mindset of abundance, aiding in letting go of negativity.

9. **Journaling for Release:**
   - Use journaling as a therapeutic practice for letting go. Write about your thoughts, feelings, and experiences, allowing the process of putting them on paper to provide a sense of release and clarity.

10. **Mindful Movement and Release:**
    - Incorporate mindful movement practices like yoga or tai chi. These activities involve intentional, flowing movements that can serve as a physical metaphor for letting go. The mindfulness in movement helps release tension and stress.

11. **Progressive Muscle Relaxation (PMR):**
    - **Focused Muscle Groups:**
    - Systematically engage various muscle groups, starting from your toes and working your way up to your head. This comprehensive approach ensures that tension is released from all areas of your body.
    - **Mind-Body Connection:**
    - Develop a heightened awareness of the mind-body connection during PMR.

      As you tense and release muscles, pay attention to the corresponding sensations, fostering a deeper understanding of physical tension and relaxation.
    - **Customized PMR Routine:**
    - Tailor your PMR routine to focus on specific areas prone to tension. This customization allows you to address individual stress patterns, creating a more personalized and effective relaxation practice.
    - **Breathing Coordination:**
    - Coordinate your breathing with muscle tension and relaxation. Inhale deeply as you tense the muscles, and exhale slowly as you release the tension. This synchronization enhances the overall relaxation response.
    - **Mindful Muscle Release:**
    - Integrate mindfulness into the muscle release phase. As you let go of tension, mindfully experience the sensation of relaxation in each muscle group, reinforcing a sense of letting go.
    - **Regular Practice for Cumulative Benefits:**
    - Make PMR a regular practice to accumulate its benefits over time.
      Consistent engagement with this technique enhances your ability to release tension at will, contributing to a more relaxed overall state.

12. **Visualization for Release:**
    - Use visualization techniques to mentally let go of stressors. Envision placing your worries in a balloon and watching it float away, symbolizing the act of releasing burdens.
13. **Developing a Detached Observer Mindset:**
    - Cultivate a detached observer mindset by viewing situations from a neutral perspective. This involves stepping back mentally, observing events without intense emotional involvement, and fostering a sense of detachment.
14. **Self-Compassion Practices:**
    - Practice self-compassion by treating yourself with kindness and understanding. Understand that imperfections and mistakes are part of being human, and self-compassion facilitates the process of accepting and letting go.
15. **Nature Connection for Grounding:**
    - Spend time in nature to gain a sense of grounding and perspective. Nature has a calming influence and can inspire a shift towards acceptance and letting go of unnecessary concerns.
16. **Mantras and Affirmations:**
    - Adopt positive mantras or affirmations that emphasize letting go and acceptance. Repeat these affirmations regularly to reinforce a mindset focused on releasing stress and embracing the present moment.
17. **Engaging in Mindful Hobbies:**
    - Pursue mindful hobbies that absorb your attention and bring joy. Activities like painting, gardening, or playing a musical instrument provide a therapeutic outlet for letting go of stress.
18. **Mindful Disconnect:**
    - Set intentional times to disconnect from technology and external stimuli. This mindful disconnect allows for mental rejuvenation and aids in releasing the constant stream of information that can contribute to stress.
19. **Constructive Distraction:**
    - Engage in constructive distractions to shift your focus. Activities that bring joy or require concentration can divert your mind from stressors, facilitating the process of letting go.
20. **Acceptance and Commitment Therapy (ACT):**
    - Explore Acceptance and Commitment Therapy principles, which emphasize accepting what is beyond your control and committing to actions aligned with your values. ACT techniques help in letting go of struggles with unchangeable circumstances.

Part Five:
Strategies for the Mind

Chapter 1

Cognitive Restructuring:
Changing Your Thoughts

1. **Identifying Irrational Beliefs:**
   - **Mindfulness-Based Self-Reflection:**
   - Engage in mindfulness practices to heighten self-awareness. Mindfulness allows you to observe thoughts without immediate judgment, making it easier to identify irrational beliefs. Regular self-reflection enhances your ability to recognize and understand the nature of your thoughts.
   - **Externalizing Negative Self-Talk:**
   - Externalize negative self-talk by giving it a name or persona. This technique allows you to separate yourself from these thoughts, making it easier to analyze and challenge them objectively. For example, if the negative thought is "I'll never succeed," you can name it and say, "The self-doubt voice is speaking."
   - **Trigger Analysis:**
   - Analyze the specific triggers that lead to irrational beliefs.
     Recognizing situations, events, or interactions that prompt negative thoughts provides valuable insight into the patterns of your stressors. This awareness aids in preemptively addressing irrational beliefs.
   - **Journaling for Belief Tracking:**
   - Use a belief-tracking journal to document instances of negative or irrational beliefs. Record the context, associated emotions, and the impact these beliefs have on your behavior. Over time, patterns may emerge, enabling a more targeted approach to cognitive restructuring.
   - **Cognitive Behavioral Therapy Worksheets:**
   - Utilize Cognitive Behavioral Therapy (CBT) worksheets designed for identifying irrational beliefs. These worksheets often provide structured prompts and exercises to guide you through the process of recognizing and categorizing different types of irrational thoughts.
   - **Feedback from Trusted Individuals:**
   - Seek feedback from trusted friends, family, or colleagues.
     Others may offer valuable perspectives on your thought patterns, highlighting areas where irrational beliefs may be present. A diverse range of viewpoints can enhance your understanding of how your beliefs impact interactions.
   - **Real-Time Thought Monitoring:**
   - Implement real-time thought monitoring. Set aside specific moments during the day to consciously observe your thoughts. This can be particularly effective in catching irrational beliefs as they arise, allowing for immediate intervention and cognitive restructuring.
2. **Thought Records and Journals:**
   - Keep a thought journal to record negative thoughts and associated emotions. Analyze patterns and triggers, allowing you to pinpoint specific cognitive distortions that contribute to stress. Thought records provide a structured way to reevaluate and reframe thoughts.
3. **Reality Testing:**
   - Engage in reality testing to evaluate the accuracy of your thoughts. Ask yourself if there is concrete evidence supporting a negative belief or if you are making assumptions.
4. **The ABCD Model:**
   - **Activating Event Exploration:**
   - Dig deeper into the Activating event (A) by exploring the context and details surrounding the triggering situation. Understanding the specific elements of the event allows for a more nuanced assessment of the beliefs associated with it.
   - **Belief Interrogation:**
   - Interrogate your Beliefs (B) by questioning their rationality and validity. Challenge whether these beliefs are based on assumptions, cognitive distortions, or realistic assessments. Actively dispute irrational beliefs by introducing a constructive internal dialogue.

- **Consequence Evaluation:**
- Thoroughly evaluate the Consequences (C) of irrational beliefs. Examine the emotional and behavioral outcomes linked to these beliefs. Recognize the impact they have on your overall well-being and consider alternative responses.
- **Disputation and Reframing:**
- Engage in a structured Disputation (D) process where you actively challenge irrational beliefs. Counter negative thoughts with more balanced and realistic perspectives. Reframe the beliefs by introducing positive and constructive alternatives.
- **Cognitive Restructuring Worksheets:**
- Utilize cognitive restructuring worksheets that follow the ABCD model format. These worksheets provide a systematic approach to identifying, challenging, and reframing irrational beliefs. They act as practical tools for self-guided cognitive restructuring.
- **Visualization Techniques:**
- Incorporate visualization into the Disputation phase. Visualize scenarios where irrational beliefs are replaced with more adaptive thoughts. Visualization enhances the process of actively reshaping your cognitive responses to stressors.
- **Consistent Practice:**
- Make cognitive restructuring a consistent practice. Regularly apply the ABCD model to various stress-inducing situations. The more you practice, the more adept you become at identifying and restructuring irrational beliefs in real-time.

5. **Refuting All-or-Nothing Thinking:**
   - Challenge all-or-nothing thinking, also known as black-and-white or dichotomous thinking. Replace extreme statements like "always" or "never" with more balanced and realistic language to create a more nuanced perspective.

6. **Cognitive Restructuring Worksheets:**
   - Utilize cognitive restructuring worksheets that guide you through the process. These worksheets typically involve identifying negative thoughts, evaluating their validity, and generating alternative, more balanced thoughts.

7. **Positive Affirmations:**
   - Integrate positive affirmations into your daily routine. Affirmations are positive statements that counteract negative self-talk. Repeat these affirmations regularly to reinforce a more positive and constructive mindset.

8. **Behavioral Experiments:**
   - **Systematic Exposure Gradation:**
   - Gradually expose yourself to stress-inducing situations in a systematic and graded manner. Start with scenarios that evoke mild discomfort and progressively move towards more challenging situations. This stepwise exposure allows for a controlled exploration of negative beliefs.
   - **Outcome Documentation:**
   - Document the outcomes of behavioral experiments meticulously. Record your observations, emotional responses, and any changes in behavior. This documentation serves as concrete evidence to evaluate the accuracy of your negative beliefs and provides insights into their impact.
   - **Parallel Positive Actions:**
   - Accompany exposure to stressors with parallel positive actions. Introduce behaviors and responses that counteract the negative beliefs you are testing. This dual approach helps in creating a balanced and comprehensive view of your capabilities and coping mechanisms.
   - **Collaborative Experimentation:**
   - Engage in behavioral experiments collaboratively with a trusted friend, family member, or therapist.
     Having a supportive companion during experiments not only provides emotional support but also offers an external perspective on the validity of negative beliefs.
   - **Recorded Self-Observation:**
   - Record your observations before, during, and after behavioral experiments through audio or video recordings. This allows for a more detailed analysis of your responses and behaviors. Watching or listening to these recordings aids in gaining valuable insights into your thought patterns.

9. **Cognitive Distortion Recognition:**
   - Learn to recognize common cognitive distortions, such as overgeneralization, catastrophizing, or mind-reading. By identifying these distortions, you can interrupt automatic negative thoughts and replace them with more balanced perspectives.
10. **Gratitude Practice for Perspective Shift:**
    - Integrate a gratitude practice to shift focus from stressors to positive aspects of life. Regularly identify and appreciate things you are thankful for. This practice aids in cultivating a positive mindset and counteracting negative thought patterns.
11. **Mindfulness-Based Cognitive Restructuring:**
    - Combine mindfulness with cognitive restructuring. Mindfulness techniques can create a mental space for observing and challenging thoughts without immediate judgment, enhancing the effectiveness of cognitive restructuring.
12. **Role of Self-Compassion:**
    - Infuse self-compassion into cognitive restructuring. Treat yourself with kindness and understanding when challenging negative thoughts. Developing a supportive internal dialogue contributes to a more compassionate approach to managing stress.
13. **Thought Replacement Strategies:**
    - Develop specific strategies for replacing negative thoughts with more positive and realistic alternatives. For example, instead of saying "I can't handle this," reframe it as "I can face challenges one step at a time."
14. **Cognitive Behavioral Therapy (CBT):**
    - Consider engaging in Cognitive Behavioral Therapy (CBT). This evidence-based therapeutic approach is particularly effective for restructuring negative thought patterns and promoting healthier cognitive processes.
15. **Journaling for Thought Analysis:**
    - Use journaling as a tool for thought analysis. Write down negative thoughts, evaluate their validity, and explore alternative perspectives. Journaling provides a structured and reflective process for cognitive restructuring.
16. **Daily Positive Reflections:**
    - Integrate a daily reflection practice where you consciously acknowledge positive aspects of your day. Reflecting on positive experiences reinforces a more optimistic outlook and diminishes the impact of negative thinking.

Problem-Solving Skills
to Reduce Anxiety

1. **Define the Problem Clearly:**
   - **Contextualize the Issue:**
   - Before diving into details, understand the broader context of the problem. Consider the environment, relationships, and external factors that may contribute to or influence the issue. A holistic understanding sets the stage for targeted problem-solving.
   - **Identify Triggering Factors:**
   - Pinpoint the specific factors triggering anxiety within the defined problem. Recognizing what aspects contribute most significantly to stress allows for a more focused and strategic approach to problem resolution.
   - **Break Down into Sub-Problems:**
   - If the problem appears complex, break it down into smaller, manageable sub-problems. Each component can be addressed individually, making the overall challenge less overwhelming. This step is crucial for creating a roadmap for resolution.
   - **Distinguish Between Symptoms and Root Causes:**
   - Differentiate between the symptoms of the problem and its root causes. Symptoms are the visible manifestations, while root causes are the underlying issues. Addressing root causes directly tends to result in more sustainable solutions.
   - **Use Problem-Solving Tools:**
   - Employ problem-solving tools, such as the "5 Whys" technique, to systematically delve into the layers of the problem. By asking "why" repeatedly, you uncover deeper insights into the root causes, guiding your problem-solving efforts.
   - **Consider Multiple Perspectives:**
   - Gather input from diverse perspectives, especially if the problem involves relationships or collaborations. Different viewpoints can provide valuable insights, enriching your understanding of the issue and broadening the range of potential solutions.
   - **Define Success Criteria:**
   - Clearly articulate what success looks like in resolving the problem. Establish measurable criteria to evaluate the effectiveness of your solutions.
2. **Prioritize Concerns:**
   - **Assess Urgency and Impact:**
   - When prioritizing concerns, evaluate each issue's urgency and impact on your well-being. Consider which problems require immediate attention and which, if left unaddressed, may have a more significant negative impact.
   - **Use a Priority Matrix:**
   - Implement a priority matrix or a similar tool to visually categorize concerns based on urgency and importance. This strategic approach helps in focusing your efforts on tasks that align with both criteria.
   - **Assess Resource Availability:**
   - Evaluate the resources available to address each concern. This includes time, energy, and external support. Prioritize issues that align with your current resource capacity to ensure effective problem-solving.
   - **Celebrate Small Wins:**
   - As you address and resolve high-priority concerns, celebrate the small wins.
   - **Break Down Large Issues:**
   - If a significant concern seems overwhelming, break it down into smaller, more manageable tasks. Tackling smaller components incrementally can make the overall challenge more approachable and less stressful.

3. **Generate Multiple Solutions:**
    - Encourage creative thinking by generating a list of potential solutions to the identified problem. Avoid self-censorship during this phase, allowing for a broad range of ideas to emerge.
4. **Mind Mapping for Exploration:**
    - Use mind mapping techniques to visually explore the interconnected elements of the problem. Mind maps provide a holistic view, helping you identify root causes and potential solutions more comprehensively.
5. **Utilize External Input:**
    - Seek input from trusted friends, family, or colleagues. Other perspectives can bring fresh insights and alternative solutions that you might not have considered. Collaborative problem-solving often leads to more robust outcomes.
6. **Risk Assessment:**
    - Evaluate potential risks and benefits associated with each solution. Consider the short-term and long-term consequences, helping you make informed decisions that align with your overall well-being.
7. **Break Down Complex Issues:**
    - **Identify Key Components:**
    - Analyze the complex issue to identify its key components. Break down the problem into smaller, more manageable elements that can be addressed individually. This process helps in gaining a clearer understanding of the challenge.
    - **Prioritize Subcomponents:**
    - Once you've identified the components, prioritize them based on their interdependence, urgency, or impact. This step ensures that you focus on addressing the most crucial aspects first, leading to a systematic and strategic resolution.
    - **Create a Sequential Action Plan:**
    - Develop a sequential action plan that outlines the order in which you'll address each subcomponent.
    This plan serves as a roadmap, guiding your efforts and preventing the feeling of being overwhelmed by the entire issue.
    - **Set Milestones:**
    - Break the solution process into milestones. Establishing specific, measurable milestones provides a sense of progress and achievement. Celebrating these milestones can help maintain motivation and reduce stress associated with the larger issue.
    - **Allocate Resources Effectively:**
    - Assess the resources required for each subcomponent and allocate them strategically. This includes time, energy, knowledge, and any external support. Efficient resource allocation ensures a smoother resolution process.
    - **Seek Expert Guidance:**
    - For particularly complex issues, consider seeking guidance from experts or professionals in the relevant field. Their insights and expertise can provide valuable perspectives, helping you navigate intricate aspects of the problem more effectively.
8. **Decision-Making Criteria:**
    - Establish decision-making criteria to guide your choice among potential solutions. Consider factors such as feasibility, practicality, and alignment with your values. Having clear criteria streamlines the decision-making process.
9. **Implementation Planning:**
    - **Stakeholder Involvement:**
    - Ensure that key stakeholders are actively involved in the implementation planning process. Their insights and perspectives can provide valuable input, and involving them fosters a sense of shared responsibility for the success of the solution.
    - **Risk Assessment:**
    - Conduct a thorough risk assessment as part of the implementation planning. Anticipate potential challenges or obstacles that may arise during the execution phase. Develop contingency plans to address these risks, enhancing the resilience of the implementation process.

- **Resource Allocation:**
- Clearly define and allocate the necessary resources, including human resources, budget, technology, and materials. Ensure that each aspect of the plan has the required support to avoid delays or disruptions during implementation.
- **Communication Strategy:**
- Develop a comprehensive communication strategy to keep all relevant parties informed about the implementation process. Regular updates, progress reports, and open channels of communication contribute to transparency and stakeholder engagement.
- **Training and Development:**
- If the solution involves new processes, technologies, or skills, include a training and development component in the implementation plan. Ensure that individuals involved have the knowledge and skills required for effective execution.

10. **Progress Monitoring:**
    - Regularly monitor your progress in implementing the solution. Track both successes and challenges, and be open to adjusting your approach based on real-time feedback.

11. **Learn from Setbacks:**
    - View setbacks as opportunities for learning and improvement rather than as failures. Analyze what went wrong, adjust your strategy if needed, and use setbacks as stepping stones toward a more effective solution.

12. **Cultivate Flexibility:**
    - Remain flexible in your problem-solving approach. Sometimes, unforeseen factors may require adjustments to your initial plan. Adaptability enhances resilience in the face of challenges.

13. **Self-Reflection on Problem-Solving Style:**
    - Reflect on your preferred problem-solving style. Are you more inclined towards analytical approaches or creative brainstorming? Understanding your style allows you to tailor your problem-solving strategies to your strengths.

14. **Time Management for Problem-Solving:**
    - Allocate dedicated time for problem-solving activities. Create a conducive environment free from distractions, allowing you to focus on generating solutions and making decisions more effectively.

15. **Mindfulness and Problem-Solving:**
    - Practice mindfulness to enhance your problem-solving skills. Being fully present in the moment can sharpen your attention and cognitive abilities, fostering clearer thinking during the problem-solving process.

16. **Professional Support:**
    - If the problem is complex or emotionally charged, consider seeking professional support. A therapist or counselor can provide guidance, helping you navigate challenges and build effective problem-solving skills.

Chapter 3

Creative Visualization
and Stress

- **Understanding Creative Visualization:**
  - **Midday Reset Visualization:**
  - Incorporate a brief midday visualization to reset and recharge. Picture a moment of tranquility or accomplishment to break up the day positively. This mini-visualization can serve as a mindfulness break, enhancing focus and resilience.
  - **Specific Goal Visualization:**
  - Tailor your morning visualization to focus on a specific goal or challenge you anticipate during the day. Visualize yourself navigating through it successfully, fostering a proactive and confident mindset.
  - **Gratitude Visualization:**
  - Dedicate a visualization session to gratitude. Picture the people, experiences, and achievements you're grateful for. This gratitude-focused visualization can instill a sense of positivity and appreciation in daily life.
  - **Visualization Affirmations:**
  - Integrate positive affirmations into your visualizations.
    As you imagine scenarios, include affirmations that reinforce your capabilities, strengths, and resilience. This dual approach combines the power of visualization with positive self-talk.
  - **Body-Mind Connection Visualization:**
  - Extend your visualization to include the connection between your mental and physical well-being. Visualize a state of physical well-being, imagining energy, vitality, and a sense of balance. This holistic approach reinforces the mind-body connection.
  - **Adaptive Visualization for Challenges:**
  - If facing a specific challenge, engage in an adaptive visualization. Picture yourself approaching the challenge with flexibility and creativity. Visualize various scenarios of successful problem-solving, preparing your mindset for adaptability.
  - **Mindful Breath Integration:**
  - Infuse mindful breathing into your visualizations. Sync your breath with the imagined scenes, enhancing the mind's receptivity to relaxation cues. This integration supports a calm and centered state during the visualization process.
  - **Visualization Reflection Journal:** Maintain a visualization reflection journal. After each visualization, jot down your emotions, insights, and any shifts in mindset. This reflective practice deepens self-awareness and helps track the impact of visualization over time.
- **Guided Imagery Techniques:**
  - **Personalized Imagery Scripts:**
  - Develop personalized guided imagery scripts tailored to individual preferences and stressors. This customization allows individuals to create mental scenarios that resonate with their unique sources of relaxation and joy, promoting a more profound sense of calm.
  - **Multisensory Engagement:**
  - Encourage the engagement of multiple senses during guided imagery. In addition to visualizing scenes, incorporate sounds, textures, and scents. For example, imagine the sound of ocean waves, the warmth of sunlight, or the scent of blooming flowers. This multisensory approach enhances the immersive experience.
  - **Time-Travel Imagery:**
  - Explore time-travel imagery, where individuals mentally transport themselves to a past moment of joy or a future scenario where they've achieved their aspirations. This technique allows for a positive connection with one's history or a hopeful anticipation of the future, fostering a sense of purpose.

- **Symbolic Imagery:**
- Introduce symbolic imagery by associating specific symbols with emotions or challenges. For instance, envision releasing balloons representing worries into the sky. This symbolic visualization can provide a tangible and emotionally resonant way of addressing stressors.
- **Creative Visualization Journal:**
- Encourage individuals to maintain a creative visualization journal. This journal can serve as a personal repository for positive imagery and reflections. Regularly recording and revisiting positive visualizations contribute to building a mental reservoir of stress-relieving imagery.
- **Interactive Visualization Workshops:**
- Facilitate interactive visualization workshops where individuals can share and co-create guided imagery experiences. This communal approach fosters a sense of shared relaxation and provides an opportunity for collective creativity in stress management.
- **Goal Setting through Visualization:**
  - **Clear Goal Definition:**
  - Clearly define the goals you want to achieve. Whether they are related to personal development, career success, or stress reduction, articulate them precisely.
  - **Mental Rehearsal:**
  - Use creative visualization to mentally rehearse the process of achieving your goals. Picture each step, visualize potential challenges, and see yourself overcoming them.
- **Scripting Your Desired Reality:**
  - **Written Visualization:**
  - Write a detailed script or narrative describing your desired reality. Include sensory details, emotions, and specific achievements. Read this script regularly to reinforce the visualization process.
- **Daily Visualization Rituals:**
  - **Theme-Based Visualizations:**
  - Introduce theme-based visualizations to align with specific goals or intentions. For instance, dedicate certain days to visualizing professional success, while others may focus on personal relationships or health. This thematic approach allows for a holistic exploration of various aspects of life.
  - **Progressive Day Visualization:**
  - Expand daily visualizations into a progressive day narrative. Instead of visualizing only the beginning and end, guide individuals through mental scenarios of successfully navigating different situations and maintaining a positive mindset throughout the day.
  - **Integration with Mindful Practices:**
  - Integrate visualization rituals with other mindful practices, such as meditation or deep breathing exercises. Begin or conclude visualization sessions with moments of mindfulness, creating a seamless transition between focused imagery and present-moment awareness.
  - **Visualization Affirmations:**
  - Combine visualization with positive affirmations. As individuals visualize success and positive outcomes, encourage them to articulate corresponding affirmations aloud or internally. This verbal reinforcement enhances the impact of the visualization and contributes to a more affirming self-dialogue.
  - **Interactive Group Visualization:**
  - Facilitate group visualization sessions where individuals collectively contribute to the visualization narrative. This collaborative approach fosters a shared positive energy and a sense of community. Group visualizations can be particularly beneficial in professional or educational settings.
  - **Guided Audio Visualizations:**
  - Explore guided audio visualizations as a complement to silent visualization. Providing pre-recorded audio guidance can be helpful for individuals who prefer external prompts. Audio visualizations can incorporate calming music, nature sounds, or guided instructions to enhance the immersive experience.
- **Visualization and Stress Reduction:**
  - **Stress Release Imagery:**

- Develop mental imagery that represents stress leaving your body. This could involve visualizing tension melting away or stress transforming into a dissipating cloud.
  - **Creating a Mental Safe Space:**
- During stressful moments, retreat to your mental sanctuary through visualization. This provides a mental escape and a brief respite from stressors.
- **Enhancing Creativity and Problem-Solving:**
  - **Creative Scenario Exploration:**
- Use visualization to explore creative solutions to challenges. Picture different scenarios and outcomes to stimulate innovative thinking.
  - **Mind Mapping Imagery:**
- Visualize complex ideas or projects as mind maps. This mental imagery aids in organizing thoughts and seeing connections between different elements.
- **Combining Visualization with Affirmations:**
  - **Positive Affirmation Integration:**
- Combine positive affirmations with visualization to reinforce desired beliefs. For example, visualize success while repeating affirmations related to confidence and capability.
- **Visualization Apps and Resources:**
  - **Guided Visualization Apps:** Explore apps or resources that offer guided visualization sessions. These can provide structure and guidance, making it easier for beginners to incorporate visualization into their routine.
- **Consistency and Practice:**
  - **Scheduled Visualization Sessions:**
- Establish a consistent schedule for visualization sessions. Whether it's in the morning, during breaks, or before bedtime, having dedicated times enhances routine and ensures regular practice.
  - **Progressive Complexity:**
- Gradually increase the complexity of your visualizations. Start with simple scenes and progressively incorporate more intricate details.
  This progression challenges the mind and enhances its ability to create vivid and detailed imagery.
  - **Adapting Duration:**
- Tailor the duration of your visualization sessions to your preferences and schedule. While shorter sessions can be effective for daily maintenance, occasionally indulge in longer sessions for a more profound exploration of your visualizations.
  - **Adaptive Techniques:**
- Experiment with different visualization techniques. Explore guided visualizations, self-guided scenes, and variations in sensory details. Adapting techniques prevents monotony and keeps the practice engaging and dynamic.
  - **Mindful Transition Moments:**
- Integrate visualization into transition moments during the day. Use short visualization exercises during transitions between tasks or activities. These brief moments contribute to cumulative practice and serve as mindful pauses.

Maintaining Focus in a World of Distractions

1. **Mindful Awareness of Distractions:**
   - **Sensory Awareness Practices:**
   - Engage in sensory awareness exercises to heighten your perception of the environment.
   - Focus on each of your senses individually, noting sights, sounds, smells, textures, and tastes.
   - **Mindful Listening Techniques:**
   - Practice mindful listening to tune into the sounds around you without judgment.
   - Distinguish between background noise and significant sounds, enhancing your auditory awareness.
   - **Visual Clutter Reduction:**
   - Streamline your visual field by decluttering your workspace.
   - Minimize unnecessary items or decorations that may divert your attention.
   - **Digital Minimalism:**
   - Apply principles of digital minimalism by organizing and decluttering your digital devices.
   - Remove unused apps, files, or icons from your digital workspace to reduce visual distractions.
   - **Mindful Movement Observations:**
   - Observe your own movements mindfully, especially during periods of potential distraction.
   - Notice when you start shifting focus and redirect your attention to the present moment.
   - **Reflective Environment Assessment:**
   - Periodically reflect on your work environment's impact on your focus.
   - Consider how changes in lighting, seating, or overall setup influence your ability to concentrate.
   - **Mindful Eating Practices:**
   - Extend mindfulness to your eating habits, being fully present during meals.
   - Avoid multitasking while eating, allowing yourself to savor each bite without distraction.
   - **Cultivating Peripheral Vision Awareness:**
   - Develop awareness of your peripheral vision to detect movements or changes in your surroundings.
   - Peripheral vision can serve as an early warning system for potential distractions.
2. **Intentional Task Prioritization:**
   - Prioritize tasks based on importance and urgency to focus on critical responsibilities.
   - Utilize productivity frameworks like the Eisenhower Matrix for strategic task prioritization.
3. **Structured Time Blocking:**
   - Allocate specific time blocks for focused work without interruptions.
   - Communicate your time blocks to minimize external distractions during designated focus periods.
4. **Digital Detox Strategies:**
   - **Notification Management:**
   - Customize notification settings to receive only essential alerts during work hours.
   - Disable non-essential app notifications to minimize interruptions.
   - **Designated Tech-Free Zones:**
   - Establish specific areas, such as your bedroom or dining table, as tech-free zones.
   - This creates dedicated spaces for relaxation and interpersonal connection without digital distractions.
   - **Unplug Before Bed:**
   - Implement a routine of disconnecting from electronic devices at least an hour before bedtime.
   - Reduce exposure to screens to promote better sleep quality and enhance overall well-being.
   - **Screen-Free Meals:**
   - Designate meal times as screen-free to encourage mindful eating and social interaction.
   - Avoid the temptation to check devices while enjoying your meals.
   - **Mindful Tech Consumption:**
   - Practice mindful consumption of digital content.

- Be intentional about the quality and purpose of the content you engage with, avoiding mindless scrolling.
- **Digital Sabbath:**
- Dedicate a specific day or part of a day as a digital Sabbath, where you completely disconnect from all digital devices.
- Use this time for activities that promote relaxation, creativity, and in-person connections.
- **Create Offline Rituals:**
- Develop offline rituals that signal the beginning or end of your workday.
- Engage in activities like reading a physical book, journaling, or taking a nature walk without digital distractions.
- **Tech-Free Hobbies:**
- Cultivate hobbies that don't involve digital devices.
- Whether it's painting, gardening, or playing a musical instrument, having tech-free hobbies provides a mental break from screens.

5. **Single-Tasking Practices:**
   - Embrace single-tasking over multitasking to enhance concentration.
   - Complete tasks sequentially to promote a sense of accomplishment and minimize distractions.
6. **Mindfulness-Based Focus Techniques:**
   - Incorporate mindfulness practices such as mindful breathing to redirect attention.
   - Practice brief mindfulness exercises when distractions arise to regain focus.
7. **Physical Environment Optimization:**
   - Organize and optimize your workspace for minimal distractions.
   - Personalize your environment with elements that inspire focus, such as plants or calming colors.
8. **Establishing Clear Boundaries:**
   - **Effective Communication:**
   - Clearly communicate your work hours and periods of focused concentration to those around you.
   - Express the importance of uninterrupted time for optimal productivity and stress management.
   - **Set Expectations with Family:**
   - Discuss and set expectations with family members about when you'll be available and when you need focused work time.
   - Clearly communicate specific hours or blocks of time dedicated to work-related tasks.
   - **Create a Designated Workspace:**
   - Establish a designated workspace that signals when you are in "work mode."
   - Use this space consistently to create a physical boundary between work and personal life.
   - **Utilize Technology for Boundaries:**
   - Leverage technology to set virtual boundaries, such as updating your status on communication platforms to indicate focused work.
   - Utilize scheduling features to automate notifications about your availability.
   - **Regular Check-ins:**
   - Plan regular check-ins with family or colleagues to maintain open communication.
   - This allows for adjustments to the schedule or addressing urgent matters without compromising the overall focus.
   - **Flexible Scheduling:**
   - Embrace flexibility in your schedule to accommodate both work and personal commitments.
   - Establish clear boundaries for focused work but remain adaptable to unexpected situations or family needs.
   - **Share a Calendar:**
   - Share your work calendar with family or housemates to make them aware of your scheduled focused work hours.
9. **Regular Breaks for Refreshment:**
   - Integrate strategic breaks into your work routine for mental refreshment.
   - Engage in brief activities during breaks, such as stretching or mindfulness exercises.
10. **Goal-Oriented Planning:**
    - Set clear, achievable goals for each work session to provide a roadmap.
    - Define the desired outcome of your work, aligning tasks with overarching goals.

11. **Cultivating Deep Work Habits:**
    - Dedicate specific periods to deep work without interruptions.
    - Develop rituals to signal the beginning and end of deep work sessions.
12. **Adapting to External Challenges:**
    - Acknowledge and adapt to unexpected interruptions or changes.
    - Develop resilience by embracing adaptability and quickly refocusing on tasks.
13. **Mindful Handling of Notifications:**
    - Disable non-essential notifications during focused work.
    - Implement the two-minute rule for quick responses, deferring longer tasks to designated times.
14. **Reflective Evaluation and Adjustment:**
    - Regularly evaluate focus strategies and make adjustments based on effectiveness.
    - Solicit feedback from colleagues or mentors to refine your approach.
15. **Incorporating Visual Cues:**
    - Use visual cues like a dedicated workspace or specific attire for focused work.
    - These cues create mental associations, signaling the importance of the task at hand.
16. **Implementing the Pomodoro Technique:**
    - Break work into intervals (typically 25 minutes) separated by short breaks.
    - This structured approach helps maintain focus and productivity.
17. **Utilizing Noise-Canceling Devices:**
    - Invest in noise-canceling headphones or devices to minimize auditory distractions.
    - Create a quiet environment conducive to concentration.
18. **Setting Realistic Expectations:**
    - Establish realistic expectations for task completion.
    - Avoid overcommitting to tasks, which can lead to stress and increased susceptibility to distractions.
19. **Collaborative Time Management:**
    - Collaborate with colleagues to synchronize focused work periods.
    - This synchronized approach reduces the likelihood of external disruptions.
20. **Mindful Email Management:**
    - Set specific times to check and respond to emails.
    - Avoid constant email monitoring to prevent interruptions and maintain focus.

Part Six:
Physical Wellness

Movement as Medicine: Exercise and Stress

- **Mindful Cardiovascular Exercise:**
  - **Nature Connection:**
  - Incorporate cardiovascular exercise in natural settings like parks or trails. Connecting with nature during activities such as trail running or hiking enhances the mindfulness experience. The changing scenery and fresh air contribute to stress reduction.
  - **Breath Synchronization:**
  - Sync your breath with your cardiovascular activity. Coordinate your inhales and exhales with your strides or pedal strokes. This mindful approach helps regulate your breathing patterns, promoting relaxation and reducing stress.
  - **Body Scan while Moving:**
  - Practice a body scan technique while engaging in cardiovascular exercise. Focus your attention on different parts of your body, from your head to your toes. This promotes a heightened awareness of your body's movements, enhancing the overall mindfulness experience.
  - **Intuitive Movement:**
  - Allow your body to guide your movements during cardiovascular exercise. Instead of sticking to a rigid routine, tune in to how your body feels and adjust your intensity accordingly. This intuitive approach fosters a deeper connection between your body and mind.
  - **Mindful Playlist Selection:**
  - Curate a mindful playlist for your cardiovascular workouts. Choose music that complements the rhythm of your exercise and enhances the overall experience. This can contribute to a more immersive and stress-relieving session.
  - **Variety in Cardiovascular Activities:**
  - Introduce variety into your cardiovascular routine. Switch between different activities such as running, swimming, or cycling. Exploring diverse exercises keeps your routine interesting, preventing monotony and promoting mental engagement.
- **Progressive Muscle Relaxation through Stretching:**
  - Combine stretching exercises with progressive muscle relaxation techniques.
  - Stretching helps release tension from muscles, and when combined with conscious relaxation, it becomes a powerful stress-relieving practice. Focus on different muscle groups, allowing them to relax as you stretch.
- **Balanced Strength Training:**
  - Include strength training exercises in your routine. A well-balanced strength training program can improve overall physical resilience, enhance mood through the release of endorphins, and contribute to better stress management. Incorporate exercises targeting major muscle groups.
- **Mind-Body Connection in Yoga:**
  - Explore the mind-body connection through yoga. Yoga combines physical postures, breath control, and meditation, fostering a holistic approach to health. The meditative aspects of yoga can be particularly effective in calming the mind and reducing stress.
- **Nature Immersion with Outdoor Activities:**
  - **Forest Bathing (Shinrin-Yoku):**
  - Practice the Japanese tradition of forest bathing, known as Shinrin-Yoku. Engage in a mindful, slow-paced walk in a forested area. Immerse yourself in the sights, sounds, and scents of the forest.
    This intentional connection with nature has been associated with reduced stress and increased well-being.

- **Grounding Exercises:**
- Incorporate grounding exercises during outdoor activities. Stand or walk barefoot on natural surfaces like grass, sand, or soil. This practice, known as earthing, is believed to facilitate a connection with the Earth's energy and contribute to stress reduction.
- **Mindful Observation:**
- Practice mindful observation of your surroundings during outdoor activities. Notice the colors, textures, and movements around you. Engaging your senses in this way enhances the meditative quality of your experience, promoting relaxation and stress relief.
- **Multi-Sensory Engagement:**
- Engage multiple senses during outdoor activities. Listen to the sounds of nature, feel the warmth of sunlight, and appreciate the scents carried by the breeze. This multi-sensory approach enhances the overall sensory experience, contributing to a sense of peace and tranquility.
- **Adventure and Exploration:**
- Infuse a spirit of adventure into outdoor activities. Explore new trails, discover hidden spots, or try different outdoor sports. The element of novelty and exploration can add excitement to your experiences and elevate the positive impact on stress reduction.
- **Social Connection in Nature:**
- Combine outdoor activities with social connections. Invite friends or family to join you for a hike, picnic, or outdoor workout. Socializing in a natural setting strengthens the sense of community and amplifies the stress-relieving benefits of both nature and social interaction.
- **Dance for Emotional Expression:**
  - Incorporate dance into your routine as a form of emotional expression. Dance allows you to release pent-up emotions, express yourself creatively, and enjoy the physical benefits of movement. Consider joining dance classes or simply dancing freely to your favorite music.
- **Breathing Techniques during Exercise:**
  - Integrate intentional breathing techniques into your exercise routine.
  Coordinate your breath with movements, such as inhaling during the concentric phase and exhaling during the eccentric phase. This synchronization promotes relaxation and focuses the mind.
- **Functional Movements for Everyday Life:**
  - **Bodyweight Exercises:**
  - Integrate bodyweight exercises like squats, lunges, and push-ups into your routine. These movements engage multiple muscle groups, promoting strength and flexibility essential for daily activities.
  - **Core Strengthening:**
  - Prioritize exercises that target core strength, such as planks and stability exercises. A strong core enhances stability, posture, and overall body functionality, contributing to a resilient and well-balanced physique.
  - **Mobility Drills:**
  - Include mobility drills that focus on joint flexibility and range of motion. Movements like hip circles, shoulder rolls, and neck stretches help maintain fluidity in your movements, reducing stiffness and promoting ease in daily tasks.
  - **Balancing Exercises:**
  - Practice balancing exercises to improve stability and coordination. Activities like single-leg stands or yoga poses challenge your balance, translating to enhanced stability in activities such as walking, climbing stairs, or reaching for objects.
  - **Functional Resistance Training:**
  - Incorporate resistance training using functional movements that simulate real-world activities. For example, using resistance bands for pulling or pushing movements mimics the actions required in daily life, promoting strength in those specific patterns.
  - **Flexibility Training:**
  - Dedicate time to flexibility training, emphasizing stretches that target major muscle groups. Improved flexibility reduces the risk of injuries and enhances your ability to move comfortably through various ranges of motion in daily life.

- **Socially Connected Activities:**
  - Engage in physically active, socially connected activities.
    Whether it's joining a group fitness class, playing a team sport, or participating in recreational activities with friends, the social aspect enhances the overall experience and contributes to stress relief.
- **Mindful Walking Meditation:**
  - **Conscious Breath Integration:**
  - Combine conscious breathing with mindful walking. Sync your breath with your steps, inhaling and exhaling in rhythm. This integration of breath and movement deepens the meditative aspect of walking, promoting relaxation and stress reduction.
  - **Focus on Sensations:**
  - Direct your attention to the sensations in your feet as they make contact with the ground. Notice the shifting weight, the pressure on different parts of your foot, and the subtle movements involved. This focused awareness enhances the mind-body connection.
  - **Observation of Surroundings:**
  - Expand your awareness to the environment around you.
    Observe the sights, sounds, and smells as you walk. Engaging your senses in the present moment fosters a connection with your surroundings, contributing to a sense of calm and mindfulness.
  - **Mantra or Affirmation Walking:**
  - Introduce a mantra or positive affirmation during your walking meditation. Repeat a calming phrase with each step. This practice helps anchor your mind, redirecting it from stressors to a more positive and centered state.
  - **Variations in Walking Speed:**
  - Experiment with variations in walking speed. Start with a slow, deliberate pace and gradually transition to a faster pace. Adjusting your speed mindfully can have different effects on your mental state, from grounding to invigorating.
  - **Walking Labyrinth Meditation:**
  - If available, explore walking meditation in a labyrinth. Labyrinths offer a winding path that encourages contemplation and focused movement. Walking the labyrinth mindfully can be a symbolic journey toward stress relief and self-discovery.
  - **Body Scan Integration:**
  - Integrate a body scan practice into your walking meditation. As you walk, bring awareness to different parts of your body. Notice any tension or areas of comfort. This combination of movement and body scan enhances overall mindfulness and relaxation.
  - **Nature Connection:**
  - Choose natural settings for your mindful walking meditation. Walking in a park, garden, or along a nature trail adds the therapeutic benefits of nature to your meditative practice. The combination of movement and natural surroundings enhances stress reduction.
  - **Mindful Transitions:**
  - Use walking meditation as a mindful transition between activities. Whether it's during a work break or a shift from one environment to another, incorporating mindful walking into transitions creates moments of centeredness and calm amidst daily demands.

The Importance of Restorative Sleep

1. **Establish a Consistent Sleep Schedule:**
   - Stick to a regular sleep-wake cycle by going to bed and waking up at the same time every day, even on weekends.
2. **Create a Relaxing Bedtime Routine:**
   - **Aromatherapy:**
   - Incorporate calming scents into your bedtime routine. Essential oils like lavender or chamomile can be diffused or applied to promote relaxation.
   - **Soft Music or Nature Sounds:**
   - Listen to soft and soothing music or nature sounds to create a serene atmosphere. This can help transition your mind from the busyness of the day to a more tranquil state.
   - **Progressive Muscle Relaxation (PMR):**
   - Include PMR as part of your bedtime routine. Systematically tense and then relax different muscle groups to release physical tension.
   - **Yoga or Gentle Stretching:**
   - Practice gentle yoga or stretching exercises to release physical tension and promote flexibility. Focus on slow and deliberate movements.
   - **Warm Beverage Ritual:**
   - Develop a ritual of sipping on a warm, caffeine-free beverage like herbal tea or warm milk. This can have a comforting and calming effect.
   - **Guided Meditation:**
   - Listen to guided meditation specifically designed for bedtime. This can guide your mind into a state of relaxation and prepare it for sleep.
   - **Create a Comfortable Sleep Environment:**
   - Ensure your sleep environment is comfortable and conducive to relaxation. This includes adjusting room temperature, using comfortable bedding, and creating a clutter-free space.
   - **Reading Positive Affirmations:**
   - Read or recite positive affirmations before bedtime to foster a positive mindset and ease any lingering stress or negative thoughts.
3. **Optimize Sleep Environment:**
   - Ensure your bedroom is conducive to sleep by keeping it cool, dark, and quiet. Invest in comfortable bedding and pillows.
4. **Limit Exposure to Screens Before Bed:**
   - **Blue Light Filters:**
   - Install blue light filters on electronic devices or use apps that reduce blue light emission in the evening. This can lessen the impact on melatonin levels.
   - **Night Mode on Devices:**
   - Activate the "Night Mode" or similar features on your devices. These settings adjust the screen colors to warmer tones, reducing the stimulating effects of blue light.
   - **Read a Physical Book:**
   - Instead of reading from a digital device, opt for a physical book. The absence of a screen can enhance the calming effect of reading before bed.
   - **Set Screen Time Limits:**
   - Use built-in features or third-party apps to set screen time limits on your devices. This helps you adhere to a pre-determined schedule for winding down.
   - **Create a Charging Station Outside the Bedroom:**
   - Charge electronic devices outside the bedroom to resist the temptation of checking messages or using screens right before sleep. This supports a screen-free sleep environment.

- **Invest in Blue Light Blocking Glasses:**
- Consider using blue light blocking glasses, especially if it's challenging to avoid screens in the evening. These glasses can mitigate the impact of blue light on melatonin production.
- **Engage in Non-Screen Activities:**
- Choose non-screen activities for the hour before bed. This could include listening to soothing music, practicing relaxation exercises, or engaging in light stretching.
- **Dim Ambient Lighting:**
- Dim the ambient lighting in your living space during the evening. This prepares your body for sleep and reduces the overall exposure to artificial light.
- **Use Physical Alarm Clocks:**
- Instead of relying on your phone as an alarm, use a physical alarm clock.
- **Establish a Charging Routine:**
- Charge electronic devices in a specific location and establish a routine of putting them on charge well before bedtime. This ritual can help disconnect from screens intentionally.
- **Familiarize Yourself with E-Reader Settings:**
- If you use an e-reader, familiarize yourself with settings that minimize blue light emission. Some e-readers have features similar to blue light filters found on smartphones.

5. **Mindful Breathing for Relaxation:**
   - Practice mindful breathing exercises before bedtime to calm the nervous system and signal the body that it's time to wind down.
6. **Avoid Stimulants Before Bed:**
   - Limit caffeine and nicotine intake in the evening, as these can disrupt sleep patterns.
7. **Light Exposure During the Day:**
   - Spend time outdoors during daylight hours to regulate your circadian rhythm and enhance natural sleep-wake cycles.
8. **Limit Naps:**
   - If you need to nap, keep it short (20-30 minutes) and avoid napping too close to bedtime.
9. **Evaluate Mattress and Pillows:**
   - Ensure your mattress and pillows provide adequate support and comfort. Replace them if they are worn out.
10. **Manage Stress and Anxiety:**
    - **Mindfulness Meditation Before Bed:**
    - Engage in mindfulness meditation specifically designed for bedtime. Focus on your breath and let go of racing thoughts, promoting a calm mental state conducive to sleep.
    - **Guided Imagery for Relaxation:**
    - Explore guided imagery exercises aimed at relaxation. Visualize peaceful scenes or scenarios that evoke feelings of tranquility, helping to shift your mind away from stressors.
    - **Journaling for Stress Release:**
    - Establish a pre-sleep journaling routine. Write down any lingering thoughts, worries, or to-do lists to release them from your mind, reducing the mental burden before bedtime.
    - **Progressive Muscle Relaxation (PMR):**
    - Incorporate a detailed PMR session into your bedtime routine. Systematically tense and then relax each muscle group, promoting physical and mental relaxation.
    - **Deep Breathing Techniques:**
    - Practice deep breathing exercises specifically tailored for stress reduction. Techniques such as diaphragmatic breathing or 4-7-8 breathing can calm the nervous system and alleviate tension.
    - **Body Scan Meditation for Relaxation:**
    - Integrate body scan meditation as a tool for relaxation. Direct your focus to different parts of your body, releasing tension and promoting a sense of ease before sleep.
    - **Aromatherapy for Relaxing Scents:**
    - Use calming scents through aromatherapy, such as lavender or chamomile. Essential oils or diffusers can create a soothing environment that helps manage stress and enhances sleep quality.
    - **Relaxing Music or Nature Sounds:**

- Incorporate relaxing music or nature sounds into your pre-sleep routine. Create a playlist of calming tunes or sounds of nature to drown out stress-inducing noises and foster a serene atmosphere.

11. **Physical Activity During the Day:**
    - Engage in regular physical activity, but avoid intense exercise close to bedtime. Moderate exercise can promote better sleep.

12. **Cognitive Behavioral Therapy for Insomnia (CBT-I):**
    - Consider CBT-I, a structured program that addresses the thoughts, behaviors, and attitudes affecting sleep.

13. **Use White Noise or Relaxing Sounds:**
    - White noise or calming sounds can drown out disruptive background noise and create a soothing sleep environment.

14. **Limit Liquid Intake Before Bed:**
    - Minimize the consumption of liquids in the evening to reduce the likelihood of waking up for bathroom trips.

15. **Address Sleep Disorders:**
    - If you suspect a sleep disorder, such as sleep apnea or insomnia, seek professional evaluation and treatment.

16. **Herbal Teas for Relaxation:**
    - Drink caffeine-free herbal teas like chamomile or valerian root, known for their relaxing properties.

17. **Journaling Before Bed:**
    - Write down thoughts or concerns in a journal before bed to clear your mind and reduce bedtime anxiety.

18. **Avoid Heavy Meals Before Bed:**
    - Opt for a light snack if you're hungry before bed. Avoid heavy meals, which can cause discomfort.

19. **Limit Clock Watching:**
    - Turn clocks away from view to prevent clock-watching, which can create stress and anxiety about the time.

20. **Progressive Muscle Relaxation (PMR):**
    - Practice PMR to systematically relax different muscle groups, promoting overall physical relaxation.

21. **Mindfulness Meditation for Sleep:**
    - Engage in mindfulness meditation designed specifically to induce a state of relaxation conducive to sleep.

22. **Limit Caffeine After Noon:**
    - If you consume caffeinated beverages, avoid them in the afternoon and evening to prevent interference with sleep.

23. **Explore Natural Supplements:**
    - Consider natural supplements like melatonin, magnesium, or valerian root after consulting with a healthcare professional.

24. **Establish Wind-Down Time:**
    - Dedicate a period of time before bed for winding down, avoiding stimulating activities.

Balancing Your Energy:
Understanding Your Bio-rhythms

1. **Daily Routine Alignment:**
   - **Strategic Task Planning:**
   - Organize your daily tasks strategically by prioritizing more demanding or mentally challenging activities during your peak energy hours. This ensures that important responsibilities receive your focused attention.
   - **Morning Hydration Rituals:**
   - Incorporate hydration as part of your morning routine. Drinking a glass of water upon waking can kickstart your metabolism and contribute to improved cognitive function throughout the day.
   - **Mindful Meal Preparation:**
   - Practice mindfulness while preparing and consuming your morning meal. Take the time to savor the flavors and textures, fostering a sense of presence and setting a positive tone for the day.
   - **Mindful Commuting Practices:**
   - If commuting is part of your daily routine, use this time mindfully. Listen to calming music, practice deep breathing, or engage in a brief mindfulness meditation to ease into the day.
   - **Afternoon Refresh and Reset:**
   - Plan a short break or moment of refreshment during the mid-afternoon energy dip. This could involve a brisk walk, stretching exercises, or a healthy snack to reenergize and refocus for the remaining tasks.
   - **Task Batching for Efficiency:**
   - Group similar tasks together through task batching. This allows you to tackle related activities consecutively, optimizing your focus and efficiency while minimizing mental strain.
   - **Technology Breaks for Mental Clarity:**
   - Schedule short breaks from digital devices throughout the day. This practice helps prevent cognitive fatigue and eye strain, promoting mental clarity and overall well-being.
   - **Midday Mindfulness Check-In:**
   - Incorporate a mindfulness check-in during the middle of the day.
     Take a few moments to assess your mental and emotional state, adjusting your mindset and activities as needed for a more balanced afternoon.
2. **Strategic Work Breaks:**
   - Implement the Pomodoro Technique, which involves working in focused intervals (e.g., 25 minutes) followed by a short break. This aligns with the natural ebb and flow of cognitive energy.
   - Schedule short breaks for physical movement or activities that boost energy during natural energy lulls.
3. **Circadian Rhythm Optimization:**
   - Leverage exposure to natural light, especially in the morning, to regulate circadian rhythms. Natural light positively influences mood, alertness, and sleep-wake cycles.
   - Establish a consistent nighttime routine to signal to your body that it's time to wind down. This can include dimming lights, avoiding screens, and engaging in relaxing activities.
4. **Sleep Hygiene Practices:**
   - Maintain a regular sleep schedule by going to bed and waking up at the same time each day, supporting a stable circadian rhythm.
   - Minimize screen time before bedtime to avoid disruptions to melatonin production, contributing to better sleep quality.
5. **Emotional Cycle Awareness:**
   - **Mindful Self-Reflection:** During emotionally challenging phases, practice mindful self-reflection to understand emotional responses better.

- **Communication Strategy:** Communicate openly with others about emotional cycles, fostering understanding and support during more sensitive periods.

6. **Adaptive Exercise Routine:**
   - **Variety in Workout Modalities:**
   - Incorporate a variety of exercise modalities into your routine. This could include cardio, strength training, flexibility exercises, and recreational activities. Diversity not only prevents monotony but also accommodates different energy requirements.
   - **Mindful Warm-Up and Cool Down:**
   - Begin each workout session with a mindful warm-up. Focus on gradually increasing your heart rate and joint mobility. Similarly, conclude with a thorough cool down to promote flexibility and prevent post-exercise stiffness.
   - **Energy-Boosting Pre-Workout Nutrition:**
   - Consume a balanced pre-workout snack or meal that provides sustainable energy. Include a mix of carbohydrates, protein, and healthy fats to fuel your exercise routine and enhance overall performance.
   - **Hydration as a Performance Booster:**
   - Prioritize hydration throughout the day, especially before and after exercise. Proper hydration supports optimal physical performance and aids in recovery.
   - **Periodization for Intensity Management:**
   - Implement periodization principles in your exercise routine. This involves alternating between periods of higher and lower intensity to prevent burnout and accommodate variations in energy levels over time.
   - **Intuitive Exercise Selection:**
   - Listen to your body and choose exercises intuitively based on how you feel on a given day. If you're experiencing higher energy levels, you might opt for more dynamic and challenging activities, while lower energy days may call for gentler forms of movement.
   - **Adjustable Workout Duration:**
   - Allow flexibility in the duration of your workouts.
     Some days you may have the energy for a longer session, while on others, a shorter, focused workout may be more suitable.
   - **Incorporate Active Recovery:**
   - Integrate active recovery days into your routine. These lighter exercise sessions, such as walking, swimming, or cycling at a leisurely pace, contribute to overall recovery and help maintain consistency without excessive strain.
   - **Listen to Your Body's Signals:**
   - Pay attention to signals from your body during and after exercise. If you feel fatigued or notice signs of overtraining, be willing to modify or skip a session to prioritize recovery.

7. **Intellectual Cycle Utilization:**
   - **Strategic Task Prioritization:**
   - Strategically prioritize tasks based on their intellectual demands. Identify high-priority, intellectually demanding activities and allocate them to periods when your cognitive energy is naturally at its peak.
   - **Creative Endeavors during Peak Cognition:**
   - Schedule creative endeavors and projects that require innovative thinking during phases of heightened cognitive energy. This can include activities such as brainstorming, writing, or artistic pursuits.
   - **Learning and Skill Development:**
   - Utilize high intellectual phases for learning new skills or acquiring knowledge. Engage in activities that stimulate your intellect, such as online courses, workshops, or reading complex material.
   - **Problem-Solving and Decision-Making:**
   - Reserve periods of heightened cognitive energy for problem-solving and decision-making tasks. Tackling complex issues or making important decisions during these phases can leverage your mental clarity and analytical abilities.
   - **Strategic Planning Sessions:**

- Dedicate specific time slots during intellectual peaks for strategic planning sessions. This could involve outlining goals, developing business strategies, or creating detailed plans for upcoming projects.
- **Focused Work on Analytical Projects:**
- When working on analytical projects that require attention to detail and critical thinking, align these tasks with periods of heightened cognitive function. This ensures optimal focus and precision in your work.
- **Complex Data Analysis:**
- If your work involves data analysis or processing complex information, schedule these activities during intellectual peaks. Your ability to process and interpret intricate data may be enhanced during these phases.
- **Engaging in Intellectual Hobbies:**
- Pursue intellectual hobbies or interests during high cognitive energy periods. This could include activities like solving puzzles, playing strategy games, or engaging in discussions that stimulate your intellect.
- **Collaborative Brainstorming Sessions:**
- Coordinate collaborative brainstorming sessions with colleagues or team members during intellectual peaks. Group discussions and idea generation can benefit from the collective intellectual energy of the participants.

8. **Mindfulness and Bio-rhythms:**
   - Regularly check in with your body and mind to observe bio-rhythmic fluctuations. Mindfulness practices can enhance self-awareness.
   - Be open to adapting plans mindfully when bio-rhythmic patterns indicate a need for rest or a shift in focus.

9. **Bio-rhythmic Communication:**
   - Communicate your bio-rhythmic patterns with your team or family, fostering a supportive environment that accommodates individual energy cycles.

10. **Holistic Well-being Integration:**
    - **Nutrient Timing for Energy Support:**
    - Align your meal times with energy levels to optimize nutrient absorption and digestion. Consider lighter meals during lower energy periods and more substantial, nutrient-dense meals during phases of heightened physical activity.
    - **Hydration Alignment:**
    - Coordinate your hydration habits with your daily energy cycles. Ensure adequate fluid intake during periods of increased physical activity and consider hydrating beverages with meals to support overall well-being.
    - **Mindful Eating Practices:**
    - Practice mindful eating by being present and attentive during meals. Pay attention to the flavors, textures, and sensations of the food. Mindful eating enhances the overall dining experience and supports a healthy relationship with food.
    - **Social Engagement and Connection:**
    - Schedule social interactions during periods of higher energy to enhance the quality of your connections. Engaging with others during times of increased vitality can contribute to positive social experiences and emotional well-being.
    - **Emotional Well-being Check-ins:**
    - Conduct regular emotional well-being check-ins during different energy phases. Use this self-reflection to identify emotional patterns, stressors, and areas of joy. Adjust daily activities and self-care practices based on these insights.

Yoga and Tai Chi:
Postures for Peace

1. **Mindful Movement in Yoga:**
   - Embrace the essence of yoga by focusing on mindful movement. Pay attention to the connection between breath and movement, fostering a deep sense of presence and awareness.
2. **Gentle Yoga Poses for Stress Relief:**
   - **Seated Forward Bend (Paschimottanasana):**
   - Sit with your legs stretched out in front, hinge at your hips, and reach toward your toes. This pose stretches the spine, hamstrings, and lower back, promoting a soothing release of tension.
   - **Thread the Needle (Parsva Balasana):**
   - Begin in a tabletop position, slide one arm under the other, lowering your shoulder to the mat. This pose targets the upper back and shoulders, releasing tightness and encouraging relaxation.
   - **Supported Bridge Pose (Setu Bandhasana):**
   - Lie on your back, bend your knees, and lift your hips. Place a block under your sacrum for support.
   - **Legs Up the Wall (Viparita Karani):**
   - Sit close to a wall and swing your legs up, forming an L shape. This restorative inversion stimulates relaxation, reduces fatigue, and aids in circulation, bringing a sense of calm.
   - **Reclining Butterfly Pose (Supta Baddha Konasana):**
   - Lie on your back, bring the soles of your feet together, and allow your knees to fall outward. This pose stretches the inner thighs and promotes a soothing effect on the hips.
   - **Supported Child's Pose (Balasana):**
   - Start in Child's Pose and place a bolster or cushion under your chest. Rest your forehead on the support, elongating the spine and releasing tension in the back and shoulders.
   - **Supine Twist (Supta Matsyendrasana):**
   - Lie on your back, bring one knee toward your chest, and gently guide it across your body. This twist releases tension in the spine, massages the organs, and induces a sense of relaxation.
   - **Extended Triangle Pose (Utthita Trikonasana):**
   - Stand with your legs wide apart, reach toward one foot while keeping your torso elongated. This pose stretches the sides of the body, promoting a release of tension in the waist and shoulders.
   - **Corpse Pose (Savasana):**
   - Conclude your yoga practice with Savasana. Lie on your back, legs extended, and arms relaxed by your sides. This pose allows for complete relaxation, integrating the benefits of your practice.
3. **Sun Salutations for Energy Flow:**
   - Practice Sun Salutations to promote energy flow and vitality. The sequential movements in Sun Salutations enhance circulation, flexibility, and can serve as a holistic way to start or end the day.
4. **Restorative Yoga for Deep Relaxation:**
   - Integrate restorative yoga poses that involve the use of props like bolsters and blankets. These poses, such as Legs Up the Wall or Corpse Pose, facilitate deep relaxation and stress release.
5. **Mindful Tai Chi Movements:**
   - Engage in Tai Chi, a martial art known for its slow, flowing movements. Focus on the fluidity of each motion, grounding yourself in the present moment. Tai Chi's meditative aspect contributes to stress reduction.
6. **Qi Gong for Vital Energy:**
   - Explore Qi Gong exercises within the realm of Tai Chi. These movements are designed to cultivate and balance the flow of Qi (energy) in the body, promoting a sense of vitality and calm.

7. **Breath Awareness in Yoga and Tai Chi:**
   - **Diaphragmatic Breathing (Pranayama):**
   - Integrate diaphragmatic breathing techniques into both yoga and Tai Chi practices. Emphasize deep belly breathing, allowing the diaphragm to fully expand on inhalation and contract on exhalation. This technique promotes relaxation and lowers stress levels.
   - **Ujjayi Breath (Ocean Breath):**
   - In yoga, incorporate Ujjayi breath, often referred to as the "ocean breath." This involves breathing in and out through the nose, slightly constricting the back of the throat to create a gentle sound resembling ocean waves.
   - **Nadi Shodhana (Alternate Nostril Breathing):**
   - Explore Nadi Shodhana in yoga, an alternate nostril breathing technique. This practice involves breathing through one nostril at a time, promoting balance, mental clarity, and a sense of calm. It can be particularly effective in reducing anxiety and stress.
   - **Square Breathing (Box Breathing):**
   - Implement square breathing techniques in both yoga and Tai Chi. Inhale, hold the breath, exhale, and pause, each for a count of four. This structured breathing pattern enhances concentration, calms the nervous system, and fosters relaxation.
   - **Tai Chi Breathing Coordination:**
   - In Tai Chi, synchronize breath with movements, emphasizing a natural and flowing rhythm. Connect inhalations and exhalations with specific postures, allowing the breath to guide and support the gentle, continuous motions of Tai Chi.
   - **Mindful Breathing in Yoga Poses:**
   - During yoga poses, maintain mindfulness of your breath. Focus on the inhale and exhale, allowing the breath to guide your movement.
   - **Breath-Centric Meditation:**
   - Integrate breath-centric meditation into both practices. Dedicate specific sessions to mindful breathing, either seated or lying down. Directing attention to the breath helps quiet the mind, reduce mental chatter, and induce a state of relaxation.
   - **Belly Breathing in Tai Chi Movements:**
   - In Tai Chi, emphasize belly breathing during movements. Let the breath initiate and guide each motion, fostering a harmonious flow between breath and movement. This mindful coordination enhances the meditative aspect of Tai Chi.
   - **Conscious Exhalation in Yoga Twists:**
   - During yoga twists, focus on conscious exhalation to deepen the twist and encourage release of tension. The breath becomes a tool for facilitating both physical and mental flexibility, aiding in stress relief.
8. **Yoga Nidra for Deep Relaxation:**
   - Practice Yoga Nidra, also known as yogic sleep, to induce a state of profound relaxation. This guided meditation technique in yoga can alleviate stress and promote mental clarity.
9. **Tai Chi for Balance and Harmony:**
   - Experience the balance and harmony cultivated by Tai Chi.
   The deliberate, slow movements enhance balance, coordination, and can have a calming effect on the nervous system.
10. **Mindful Transitions Between Poses:**
    - Focus on the transitions between yoga poses and Tai Chi movements. Mindful transitions enhance the meditative aspect of these practices, allowing for a seamless flow of energy and awareness.
11. **Incorporate Yoga and Tai Chi into Daily Routine:**
    - Integrate short sessions of yoga or Tai Chi into your daily routine. Consistency is key, and even brief practices can contribute significantly to stress management.
12. **Guided Classes or Videos:**
    - Utilize guided classes or online videos for structured yoga and Tai Chi sessions. Following expert guidance can deepen your practice and ensure correct technique.
13. **Community Engagement in Yoga and Tai Chi:**
    - Join local classes or online communities for yoga and Tai Chi. Sharing the practice with others enhances motivation, provides support, and fosters a sense of belonging.

14. **Mindful Eating Practices Post-Practice:**
    - Cultivate mindful eating habits after yoga or Tai Chi sessions. Pay attention to the flavors and textures of your food, extending the practice of mindfulness beyond the physical postures.
15. **Regular Check-ins with Your Body:**
    - Develop a habit of checking in with your body before, during, and after yoga or Tai Chi practice. This self-awareness promotes a deeper connection with your physical and mental state.
16. **Adapt Practices to Your Comfort Level:**
    - Modify poses and movements to suit your comfort and ability level. Both yoga and Tai Chi can be adapted to accommodate various fitness levels and physical conditions.
17. **Progressive Learning in Tai Chi:**
    - If practicing Tai Chi, consider progressive learning of forms. Gradually advancing through forms allows for a continuous challenge, contributing to a sense of accomplishment and stress reduction.
18. **Mindful Closing or Savasana:**
    - Conclude your yoga practice with a mindful closing or Savasana. Allow time for reflection and relaxation, absorbing the benefits of the practice before transitioning back into daily activities.
19. **Tai Chi as a Moving Meditation:**
    - View Tai Chi as a moving meditation. Embrace the meditative qualities of the practice, connecting breath, movement, and awareness for a holistic stress-reducing experience.
20. **Yoga and Tai Chi Retreats:**
    - Consider attending yoga or Tai Chi retreats for immersive experiences. Retreats provide an opportunity to deepen your practice in a dedicated and supportive environment.
21. **Mindfulness Walks Inspired by Tai Chi:**
    - Take mindful walks inspired by Tai Chi principles.
      Focus on the transfer of weight, the connection with the ground, and the flow of movement, enhancing your mindfulness in everyday activities.
22. **Yoga for Emotional Release:**
    - Use specific yoga poses known for emotional release. Poses like Pigeon Pose or Heart Openers can help release tension stored in the body and contribute to emotional well-being.
23. **Tai Chi for Stress-Related Tension Release:**
    - Incorporate Tai Chi movements that specifically target areas of stress-related tension. The slow and deliberate nature of Tai Chi allows for a gentle release of muscular and mental tension.
24. **Mindful Meditation After Yoga or Tai Chi:**
    - Conclude your practice with mindful meditation. Whether seated or in a comfortable lying position, dedicate time to quiet reflection, allowing the benefits of yoga or Tai Chi to integrate fully.
25. **Regular Progress Assessment:**
    - Regularly assess your progress in both yoga and Tai Chi. Celebrate improvements in flexibility, balance, and overall well-being, reinforcing the positive impact of these practices on stress management.

Part Seven:
Social Connections

Chapter 1

The Impact of Social
Support on Stress

1. **Understanding the Essence of Social Support:**
   - Social support is not just a concept; it's a lifeline that weaves through the fabric of our lives. It encompasses the strength we draw from our connections with others, a force that plays a profound role in navigating the tumultuous seas of stress.
2. **The Power of Emotional Support:**
   - **Empathetic Listening:**
   - Emotional support begins with the art of empathetic listening. Imagine a friend sitting with you, fully present, absorbing every word you share. In this attentive space, the weight of stress feels lighter as your thoughts find a compassionate listener.
   - **Non-Judgmental Understanding:**
   - Envision a safe haven where there is no judgment, only understanding. Emotional support thrives in an environment where vulnerability is embraced, and sharing one's struggles doesn't invite criticism. It's a sanctuary where authenticity is celebrated.
   - **Comfort in Shared Silence:**
   - Picture the comfort found in shared silence. Emotional support doesn't always demand words; it can manifest in the quiet companionship of someone who understands without the need for elaborate explanations. A peaceful presence that speaks volumes.
   - **The Healing Power of Presence:**
   - Imagine the healing power of someone's presence during challenging times. Emotional support is often felt in the comforting embrace of a friend, the reassuring hand on your shoulder, or the warmth of shared company. Presence becomes a tangible expression of care.
   - **Celebrating Joys Together:**
   - Emotional support extends beyond consoling during hardships; it also involves celebrating joys. Envision friends and family gathering to share in your triumphs, doubling the happiness and creating lasting memories. In these shared moments, stress loses its grip.
   - **Reciprocal Sharing of Emotions:**
   - Emotional support thrives in a reciprocal exchange of emotions.
     It's the acknowledgment that both joy and sorrow are integral parts of the human experience. In this emotional dance, individuals become pillars for each other, creating a stable foundation.
   - **Validation of Feelings:**
   - Consider the power of having your feelings validated. Emotional support involves others recognizing and acknowledging the validity of your emotions. This validation fosters a sense of being seen and heard, reducing the isolation often accompanied by stress.
   - **Creating a Safe Space:**
   - Picture the creation of a safe space where vulnerabilities can be unveiled without fear. Emotional support builds sanctuaries where individuals can express their true selves, free from the constraints of societal expectations or norms.
   - **Cultivating Emotional Intelligence:**
   - Envision a world where emotional intelligence is cultivated. Emotional support encourages the development of this intelligence, allowing individuals to navigate their own emotions and respond empathetically to others', creating a harmonious emotional ecosystem.
   - **Navigating Grief and Loss:**
   - In times of grief and loss, emotional support becomes a lifeline. Imagine a community rallying together to provide solace, empathy, and shared strength. The journey through sorrow becomes more bearable when embraced by a network of understanding hearts.
3. **Instrumental Support – A Helping Hand:**
   - Instrumental support is akin to a helping hand reaching out when we feel overwhelmed. It's the friend who lends a hand during a move, the colleague who shares the workload, or the family member who provides tangible assistance. Together, we lighten the load of life's challenges.

4. **Guidance Through Informational Support:**
   - Think of informational support as a compass that guides us through the labyrinth of uncertainties. Whether it's advice from a mentor, insights from a wise friend, or knowledge shared within a community, informational support equips us with the tools to navigate stressors.

5. **Validation and Appraisal Support:**
   - Imagine a moment of self-doubt transformed by a friend's words of affirmation or a colleague acknowledging your efforts. Appraisal support validates our experiences, fostering a sense of worth and competence, crucial pillars in the battle against stress.

6. **The Echo of Social Isolation:**
   - Close your eyes for a moment and envision facing stress without the safety net of social connections. The echo of social isolation reverberates loudly in the face of challenges, intensifying the weight of stress. It reinforces the truth – that we are inherently social beings, reliant on the comfort of shared experiences.

7. **Social Support as a Shield:**
   - Envision social support as an invisible shield that buffers the impact of life's arrows. It doesn't eliminate the challenges, but it significantly alters how we perceive and withstand them. The supportive network becomes our collective armor against the harsh winds of stress.

8. **Nurturing Bonds within Family:**
   - Consider the family as the foundational cornerstone of social support. It's where we learn the language of love, resilience, and shared responsibility. Within the family embrace, stress finds a formidable opponent.

9. **Friendships – A Sanctuary of Understanding:**
   - Friends are the comrades in the battlefield of life, standing beside us through thick and thin. In friendships, we discover a sanctuary of understanding, a space where laughter lessens the burden and shared experiences forge unbreakable bonds.

10. **Colleagues and Workplace Support:**
    - The workplace, often a terrain of stress, transforms when dotted with supportive colleagues. Imagine a team where collaboration replaces competition, where supervisors uplift rather than criticize. In such an environment, stress becomes a challenge to conquer collectively.

11. **Community Connection and Shared Strength:**
    - Zoom out to the broader canvas of community connections.
      In shared strength, we find a reservoir of support. Community ties knit together stories of resilience, turning stress into a narrative of collective triumph.

12. **Cultural Threads in the Tapestry of Support:**
    - Unravel the tapestry of support, and you'll find cultural threads intricately woven into its fabric. Cultural norms, traditions, and values shape the contours of how we seek and provide support, adding depth to the collective experience.

13. **The Digital Tapestry – Online Support:**
    - In the digital age, our tapestry extends beyond physical boundaries. Online platforms offer a virtual haven for shared experiences. From support groups to virtual communities, the digital tapestry adds new dimensions to the landscape of social support.

14. **Reciprocity – The Dance of Giving and Receiving:**
    - Envision social support as a dance of reciprocity. In giving, we receive, and in receiving, we give. This dance builds a rhythm that echoes through the corridors of relationships, creating harmonious connections.

15. **Building Bridges of Trust:**
    - Trust is the mortar that holds the bricks of social support together.
      It's the assurance that when we lean on others, we won't topple. Building bridges of trust requires vulnerability, yet it's in this vulnerability that the strongest connections are forged.

16. **Online and Offline: Blurring Boundaries:**
    - Consider the blurring boundaries between online and offline support. In this hybrid landscape, we find a spectrum of connections. From a comforting text to a face-to-face conversation, the lines between virtual and real become beautifully blurred.

17. **Seeking Professional Support – A Vital Chapter:**
    - Imagine the stigma of seeking professional support dissipating. Seeking therapy or counseling becomes a natural chapter in the book of managing stress. Professional support complements the broader narrative, offering specialized tools for intricate challenges.
18. **The Language of Supportive Communication:**
    - Picture a conversation infused with the language of support. Active listening, empathy, and non-judgmental communication create a safe space. In this space, stress loses some of its sharp edges, softened by the warmth of understanding.
19. **Navigating Storms within Relationships:**
    - Relationships, like ships, encounter storms. Yet, it's in navigating these storms together that the bonds strengthen. The ability to weather relationship challenges becomes a testament to the resilience of social support.
20. **The Ripple Effect: Spreading Support Beyond Borders:**
    - Visualize the ripple effect of support spreading beyond individual lives. The support we receive doesn't end with us; it extends its arms to touch others. In this ripple effect, the collective strength of interconnected lives becomes a force of positive change.
21. **Generational Threads of Support:**
    - Consider the passing down of generational threads of support. From grandparents to parents to children, the wisdom of navigating stress becomes an heirloom. Each generation contributes to the evolving tapestry, weaving resilience across time.
22. **Celebrating Diversity in Support Networks:**
    - Diversity paints the canvas of support networks. It's in embracing diverse perspectives, backgrounds, and experiences that the tapestry gains richness.
23. **Cultivating Trust Within Relationships:**
    - Reflect on the importance of cultivating trust within relationships. Trust ensures that individuals feel secure in sharing vulnerabilities and seeking assistance, promoting a supportive atmosphere.
24. **Balancing Independence and Interdependence:**
    - Balancing independence with interdependence is key. While autonomy is important, recognizing the value of interdependence allows individuals to lean on others when needed, promoting a healthy balance in relationships.
25. **Continual Evaluation and Adjustment:**
    - Social support strategies should be continually evaluated and adjusted. As circumstances change, individuals can reassess their support networks, seeking new connections or modifying existing relationships to better align with evolving needs.

Communicating Effectively to Reduce Conflicts

1. **Active Listening:**
   - Imagine a conversation where each word is not just heard but truly listened to. Active listening involves fully concentrating, understanding, responding, and remembering what is being said. It creates an atmosphere of respect and validation, reducing the potential for misunderstandings and conflicts.
2. **Clear and Concise Expression:**
   - **Precision in Language:**
   - Visualize communication as a well-crafted piece of art, where every word is chosen with precision. Using language that is specific and unambiguous reduces the risk of confusion and ensures that the intended message is conveyed accurately.
   - **Avoiding Ambiguity:**
   - Picture a communication landscape devoid of ambiguity. Clear expression involves steering away from vague or unclear statements that could lead to varied interpretations.
     This intentional clarity minimizes the chances of misunderstandings and promotes a shared understanding.
   - **Structured Communication:**
   - Imagine communication as a well-structured narrative. Organizing thoughts in a logical manner enhances clarity. Whether through written or spoken communication, a structured approach guides the recipient through a seamless flow of ideas, preventing confusion.
   - **Focused Message Delivery:**
   - Envision communication that is focused and to the point. Clear expression involves delivering the intended message without unnecessary elaboration or tangents. This concise approach respects the recipient's time and attention, fostering engagement and understanding.
   - **Elimination of Jargon:**
   - Picture a communication space where jargon is minimized. Clear and concise expression involves avoiding unnecessary technical or industry-specific language that might be unfamiliar to the audience. This inclusivity ensures that the message resonates with a broader audience.
   - **Clarity in Non-Verbal Communication:**
   - Visualize not only spoken or written words but also the non-verbal cues accompanying them. Clear expression extends to non-verbal communication, where gestures, facial expressions, and body language align with the verbal message, reinforcing a consistent narrative.
   - **Consideration of Context:**
   - Imagine a communication approach that is contextually aware. Clarity involves tailoring the message to the specific context, taking into account the background, knowledge, and expectations of the audience. This contextual consideration minimizes the risk of misinterpretation.
   - **Precise Articulation of Emotions:**
   - Picture emotions articulated with precision. Expressing feelings and emotions clearly helps others understand the emotional context of the message. This transparency fosters empathy and connection, reducing the potential for conflicts arising from emotional ambiguity.
   - **Concise Summarization:**
   - Envision communication that can be summarized succinctly.
     Clear expression allows for easy summarization of key points, aiding in retention and comprehension. This summarization is particularly valuable in scenarios where complex information needs to be conveyed efficiently.

3. **Empathetic Communication:**
   - Envision a communication style infused with empathy. Empathetic communication involves understanding and sharing the feelings of another. This approach fosters connection, as individuals feel acknowledged and valued, reducing the likelihood of conflicts arising from emotional disconnect.

4. **Using "I" Statements:**
   - Imagine a conversation where individuals use "I" statements instead of accusatory language. This technique involves expressing thoughts and feelings from a personal perspective, fostering open communication without placing blame. It shifts the focus from assigning fault to understanding emotions, promoting a more collaborative resolution.

5. **Non-Verbal Cues Awareness:**
   - Picture individuals attuned to non-verbal cues.
   Effective communication involves not just words but also body language, facial expressions, and gestures. Being aware of these cues enhances understanding and reduces the chances of miscommunication or misinterpretation.

6. **Cultural Sensitivity:**
   - **Cross-Cultural Empathy:**
   - Visualize a communication landscape where empathy transcends cultural boundaries. Cultural sensitivity involves cultivating cross-cultural empathy, allowing individuals to understand and resonate with the perspectives, values, and emotions of those from diverse backgrounds.
   - **Awareness of Non-Verbal Cues:**
   - Picture a communication space where non-verbal cues are interpreted with cultural awareness. Cultural sensitivity includes recognizing the variations in non-verbal communication styles across cultures. This awareness prevents misinterpretations and fosters a more nuanced understanding.

7. **Conflict Resolution Strategies:**
   - Picture a toolkit of conflict resolution strategies.
   Effective communicators are equipped with techniques such as compromise, collaboration, and finding common ground. These strategies transform conflicts into opportunities for mutual understanding and growth.

8. **Mindful Speech:**
   - Imagine communication infused with mindfulness. Mindful speech involves choosing words consciously, considering their impact. It prevents impulsive or hurtful remarks, fostering an environment of thoughtful communication that minimizes the escalation of conflicts.

9. **Setting Clear Expectations:**
   - Envision conversations where expectations are clearly communicated. Conflicts often arise when expectations are unclear or unmet. Effective communicators express their needs and expectations, reducing the likelihood of conflicts stemming from misunderstandings.

10. **Feedback, Not Criticism:**
    - Picture feedback that is constructive, not critical.
    Effective communication involves offering feedback in a way that is focused on improvement rather than blame. This approach encourages growth and collaboration while preventing conflicts rooted in defensiveness.

11. **Avoiding Assumptions:**
    - Imagine a communication style devoid of assumptions. Effective communicators refrain from making assumptions about others' thoughts or intentions. This practice prevents misunderstandings and reduces conflicts arising from misconstrued beliefs.

12. **Open-Mindedness:**
    - Envision open-minded communication. Effective communicators approach conversations with a willingness to consider different perspectives. This open-mindedness fosters understanding and reduces conflicts rooted in rigid viewpoints.

13. **Timely Conflict Addressing:**
    - Picture conflicts being addressed in a timely manner. Effective communication involves recognizing and addressing issues before they escalate. Timely intervention prevents the accumulation of grievances, reducing the intensity of conflicts.

14. **Choosing the Right Medium:**
    - Imagine selecting the most appropriate communication medium. Whether face-to-face, email, or a phone call, effective communicators choose the medium that aligns with the nature and sensitivity of the message. This consideration reduces the risk of miscommunication.
15. **Conflict De-Escalation Techniques:**
    - Envision individuals skilled in conflict de-escalation. Effective communicators understand when and how to de-escalate tense situations. Techniques like taking a break, using humor, or expressing empathy can diffuse conflicts before they intensify.
16. **Collaborative Problem-Solving:**
    - Picture collaborative problem-solving conversations. Effective communication involves approaching challenges as shared problems to be solved together. This collaborative mindset reduces conflicts by fostering a sense of unity and common purpose.
17. **Recognizing Emotional Triggers:**
    - Imagine a heightened awareness of emotional triggers.
      Effective communicators recognize their own and others' emotional triggers, steering conversations away from potential conflict zones. This emotional intelligence promotes smoother interactions.
18. **Respecting Boundaries:**
    - Envision communication that respects personal boundaries. Effective communicators are attuned to individual comfort levels and avoid invasive inquiries. Respecting boundaries reduces the likelihood of conflicts arising from discomfort.
19. **Seeking Common Ground:**
    - Picture conversations where common ground is sought. Effective communicators actively look for shared interests or values, building bridges that minimize conflicts by emphasizing connection over differences.
20. **Encouraging Open Dialogue:**
    - Envision an environment that encourages open dialogue. Effective communication involves creating spaces where individuals feel safe expressing their thoughts and concerns. Open dialogue prevents the suppression of feelings, reducing the risk of conflicts festering in silence.
21. **Conflict Prevention Through Communication Training:**
    - Picture a world where communication training is widespread. Effective communication is a learned skill, and widespread training reduces conflicts by equipping individuals with the tools to navigate conversations thoughtfully and respectfully.
22. **Balancing Assertiveness and Flexibility:**
    - Imagine a balance between assertiveness and flexibility in communication. Effective communicators assert their needs while remaining open to compromise and adaptation. This balanced approach reduces conflicts stemming from rigid positions.
23. **Crisis Communication Preparedness:**
    - Envision preparedness for crisis communication. Effective communicators anticipate potential crises and have strategies in place to address them swiftly and responsibly. Crisis preparedness minimizes conflicts that may arise from chaotic or unmanaged situations.

Chapter 3

Creating a
Supportive Network

1. **Identifying Personal Needs:**
   - Begin by reflecting on your own needs and preferences. Picture the kind of support that resonates with you. Understanding your needs is the foundation for seeking individuals who can offer meaningful support.
2. **Building Genuine Connections:**
   - **Authentic Self-Expression:**
   - Visualize a scenario where individuals express their true selves without fear of judgment. Building genuine connections involves creating a space where authenticity is valued, allowing each person to share their thoughts, feelings, and experiences openly.
   - **Shared Values and Beliefs:**
   - Envision connecting with individuals who share similar values and beliefs. Building a supportive network involves aligning with those who resonate with your core principles. Picture discussions and interactions centered around shared values, creating a foundation for understanding.
   - **Open Communication:**
   - Picture an environment where communication flows openly and honestly. Building genuine connections requires fostering a culture of open dialogue. Imagine conversations where thoughts, concerns, and ideas are exchanged freely, strengthening the bonds of trust.
   - **Empathy in Action:**
   - Envision a community where empathy is actively practiced. Building genuine connections involves understanding and resonating with the experiences of others. Picture individuals actively listening, validating emotions, and offering support with genuine empathy.
   - **Mutual Respect:**
   - Picture an atmosphere of mutual respect within your network. Building genuine connections requires respecting diverse perspectives, opinions, and backgrounds. Imagine a space where differences are acknowledged and valued.
   - **Quality Over Quantity:**
   - Visualize prioritizing quality connections over a sheer quantity of acquaintances.
     Building a supportive network involves investing time and energy in relationships that contribute meaningfully to your life. Picture a community where depth of connection takes precedence.
3. **Active Listening Skills:**
   - Picture yourself honing the skill of active listening. Actively listening to others fosters empathy and understanding, strengthening the bonds within your network. Imagine engaging in conversations where everyone feels heard and valued.
4. **Expressing Vulnerability:**
   - Envision a space where expressing vulnerability is met with empathy. Creating a supportive network involves being open about your challenges and triumphs. Picture a community where vulnerability is seen as a strength, not a weakness.
5. **Reciprocal Support:**
   - Imagine a network where support flows both ways. Creating a reciprocal support system involves not only receiving but also offering support to others. Visualize a dynamic exchange where everyone contributes to each other's well-being.
6. **Shared Goals and Aspirations:**
   - **Collective Vision:**
   - Visualize a network where individuals share a collective vision for the future. Creating a supportive community involves aligning with those who have a shared sense of purpose, contributing to a unified vision that inspires and motivates all members.
   - **Common Objectives:**

- Picture a community where common objectives drive the collaborative efforts of its members. Creating a supportive network involves identifying and working toward shared objectives, fostering a sense of cohesion and teamwork.
- **Mutual Growth:**
- Envision a network committed to mutual growth and development.
  Creating a supportive community involves connecting with individuals who are dedicated to both personal and collective advancement. Picture members actively supporting each other's journeys of growth.
- **Inspiration from Peers:**
- Visualize a network where individuals inspire and uplift each other through shared goals. Creating a supportive community involves surrounding yourself with peers who motivate and encourage, propelling everyone toward their shared aspirations.
- **Accountability Partnerships:**
- Picture a network where members hold each other accountable for reaching shared goals. Creating a supportive community involves establishing partnerships where individuals support and encourage accountability, enhancing the likelihood of goal attainment.
- **Celebrating Milestones Together:**
- Envision a community that celebrates milestones and achievements collectively. Creating a supportive network involves rejoicing in the successes of each member, reinforcing the idea that shared goals contribute to the overall success and well-being of the community.
- **Collaborative Problem-Solving:**
- Visualize a network where collaborative problem-solving is fueled by shared goals. Creating a supportive community involves tackling challenges together, leveraging the collective wisdom and resources of the network to find innovative solutions.

7. **Nurturing Trust:**
   - Envision trust as the cornerstone of your network. Building trust takes time and consistency. Picture a space where individuals feel secure, knowing that their challenges and successes are handled with care and confidentiality.

8. **Establishing Boundaries:**
   - Picture yourself setting clear boundaries within your support system. Creating a supportive network involves communicating your limits and respecting the boundaries of others. Imagine a space where everyone feels comfortable and respected.

9. **Diverse Perspectives:**
   - Envision a network that celebrates diversity. Seek connections with individuals from various backgrounds and experiences. Picture a space where diverse perspectives enrich the collective wisdom of the group.

10. **Encouraging Positive Vibes:**
    - Imagine fostering a positive and uplifting atmosphere within your network. Creating a supportive environment involves encouraging positive communication and celebrating achievements. Picture a community that thrives on optimism.

11. **Cultivating Emotional Intelligence:**
    - Picture yourself cultivating emotional intelligence. Developing awareness of your own emotions and the emotions of others enhances communication and empathy within the network. Visualize a space where emotions are acknowledged and respected.

12. **Mindful Conflict Resolution:**
    - Envision a network equipped with mindful conflict resolution skills. Conflicts may arise, but imagine a space where conflicts are addressed constructively, strengthening rather than weakening the connections within the network.

13. **Regular Check-Ins:**
    - Picture regular and meaningful check-ins with members of your network. Imagine taking the time to inquire about each other's well-being, creating a culture of continuous connection and support.

14. **Celebrating Milestones:**
    - Envision celebrating both small and significant milestones. Creating a supportive network involves acknowledging achievements and milestones, fostering a culture of encouragement and shared joy.

15. **Virtual and In-Person Connections:**
    - Picture a blend of virtual and in-person connections. In today's interconnected world, creating a supportive network extends beyond physical proximity. Imagine a space that leverages technology to maintain connections.
16. **Supportive Rituals:**
    - Imagine incorporating supportive rituals into your network. Whether it's a monthly gathering, a shared activity, or a collaborative project, envision rituals that strengthen the sense of community and support.
17. **Adapting to Change:**
    - Envision a network that adapts to the evolving needs of its members. Creating a supportive community involves flexibility and adaptability. Picture a space that accommodates life changes and challenges with resilience.
18. **Shared Resources and Information:**
    - Picture the sharing of resources and valuable information within your network. Creating a supportive community involves providing assistance and knowledge when needed, enhancing the collective well-being of all members.
19. **Online Platforms for Connection:**
    - Envision utilizing online platforms to foster connection. Creating a supportive network involves leveraging social media or dedicated platforms to stay connected, share insights, and offer support, especially in today's digital age.
20. **Mindful Presence:**
    - Picture being fully present in your interactions. Creating a supportive network involves being mindful and attentive during conversations, ensuring that each member feels heard and valued.
21. **Encouraging Self-Care Practices:**
    - Imagine encouraging and supporting self-care practices within your network. Visualize a space where individuals prioritize their well-being and inspire each other to engage in activities that promote self-care.
22. **Continuous Growth and Learning:**
    - Envision a network committed to continuous growth and learning. Creating a supportive community involves a shared dedication to personal and collective development. Picture a space where everyone contributes to the ongoing growth of the network.
23. **Strength in Diversity:**
    - Picture the strength that comes from embracing diversity. Creating a supportive network involves recognizing the unique strengths that each individual brings. Imagine a community that thrives on the richness of its diverse members.
24. **Learning and Growing Together:**
    - Envision a network that prioritizes continuous learning and growth. Creating a supportive network involves individuals committed to learning from each other's experiences and growing together. A culture of learning enriches the network's collective wisdom.

The Healing Power
of Laughter and Play

1. **Humor Journaling:**
    *   Begin a humor journal to document daily moments of laughter and play. Reflecting on these moments enhances awareness of joyous experiences.
2. **Laughter Meditation Apps:**
    *   **Guided Laughter Sessions:**
    *   Laughter meditation apps often offer guided sessions led by experienced facilitators. These sessions provide step-by-step instructions for incorporating laughter into meditation.
    *   **Customizable Laughter Routines:**
    *   Some apps allow users to customize their laughter routines based on preferences and time constraints. This flexibility ensures that individuals can tailor their laughter meditation practice to suit their needs.
    *   **Daily Laughter Reminders:**
    *   Many apps include features that send daily reminders to practice laughter meditation. These reminders encourage consistency and help integrate laughter into a daily mindfulness routine.
    *   **Progress Tracking:**
    *   Certain apps offer progress tracking features, allowing users to monitor their laughter meditation journey. Progress metrics may include frequency, duration, and the user's self-reported mood and stress levels.
    *   **Social Integration:**
    *   Apps may include social features that enable users to connect with a community of like-minded individuals practicing laughter meditation. This social integration fosters a sense of support and shared commitment to well-being.
    *   **Laughter Challenges:**
    *   To add an element of fun and motivation, some apps incorporate laughter challenges. Users can participate in challenges that encourage consistent laughter practice and share their experiences with the community.
    *   **Breathwork Integration:**
    *   Combining laughter with breathwork is a common element in these apps. They guide users on synchronized breathing techniques to enhance the overall meditative experience and relaxation.
    *   **Laughter Affirmations:**
    *   In addition to laughter exercises, apps may include positive affirmations related to joy, playfulness, and stress reduction. This dual approach enhances the psychological benefits of laughter meditation.
3. **Comedy Shows and Stand-Up:**
    *   Incorporate regular exposure to comedy shows and stand-up performances. Laughter induced by humor has therapeutic effects on the mind and body.
4. **Laughter Workshops:**
    *   Attend laughter workshops to learn specific techniques for intentional laughter, combining playfulness and breathwork.
5. **Incorporate Playful Rituals:**
    *   **Daily Gratitude Laughter:**
    *   Combine laughter with gratitude by sharing funny moments or expressing gratitude for the humor in everyday life. This ritual promotes a positive mindset.
    *   **Silly Dress-Up Days:**
    *   Designate days where you and your friends or family wear silly outfits or accessories. This lighthearted practice adds a touch of whimsy to routine activities.
    *   **Laughter Countdowns:**

- Create countdowns to exciting events or milestones with laughter. Each day, share a funny anecdote or joke related to the upcoming event, building anticipation with humor.
- **Playful Lunch Breaks:**
- Infuse playfulness into lunch breaks by incorporating games, jokes, or funny stories. This ritual transforms a regular break into a joyful and rejuvenating experience.
- **Surprise Laughter Messages:**
- Send surprise laughter messages to friends or family members. Share a funny meme, video, or joke to brighten their day and spread laughter.
- **Laughter Reflection Sessions:**
- Set aside time for laughter reflection sessions, where you discuss moments that brought joy during the day. Reflecting on laughter enhances its positive impact.
- **Playful Workspace Decor:**
- Add playful elements to your workspace, such as funny desk accessories or playful artwork. This creates a cheerful environment that encourages laughter.

6. Laughter Yoga Clubs:
- Join local laughter yoga clubs or online sessions where collective laughter becomes a shared experience, enhancing its impact.

7. Playful Mindfulness Walks:
- Integrate playful mindfulness into walks. Notice the surroundings, embrace spontaneity, and engage in light-hearted activities during the stroll.

8. Social Games Night:
- Organize a regular social games night with friends, blending playfulness, competition, and shared laughter.

9. Laughter Playlists:
- Create laughter playlists with funny videos, memes, and comedy sketches to have readily available for a quick mood boost.

10.Laughter Retreats:
- Consider attending laughter retreats that provide immersive experiences in laughter and play, creating a rejuvenating escape.

11. Playful Visualization:
- Practice playful visualization exercises, imagining scenarios that evoke laughter and joy, promoting a positive mindset.

12. Improv Classes:
- Explore improv classes to enhance spontaneous play and creativity, contributing to stress relief.

13. Laughter Challenges:
- Engage in laughter challenges with friends or online communities, encouraging a continuous exploration of humor.

14. Playful Affirmations:
- Integrate playful affirmations into daily routines, infusing positivity and humor into self-talk for a brighter outlook.

15. Laughing Yoga Nidra:
- Experience laughter yoga nidra, combining the benefits of laughter yoga with the deep relaxation of yoga nidra.

16. Silly Dress-Up Days:
- Organize occasional silly dress-up days at work or with friends, embracing the joy of playfulness.

17. Host a Comedy Night:
- Host a comedy night at home, inviting friends to share funny stories or jokes for an evening filled with laughter.

18. Playful Art and Creativity:
- Channel playfulness through artistic expression, engaging in activities like doodling, painting, or creative writing.

19. **Laughter Challenges:** -
    - Engage in laughter challenges with friends or online communities, encouraging a continuous exploration of humor.
20. **Playful Affirmations:**
    - **Morning Mirror Pep Talks:**
    - Start your day with a burst of positivity by looking in the mirror and reciting playful affirmations. This ritual sets a cheerful tone for the day ahead.
    - **Affirmation Sticky Notes:**
    - Place playful affirmation sticky notes in strategic locations – on your mirror, computer, or fridge. These surprise reminders bring moments of joy throughout the day.
    - **Playful Affirmation Journaling:**
    - Create a dedicated journal for playful affirmations. Regularly jot down humorous and uplifting affirmations to reflect on during moments of self-reflection.
    - **Affirmation Alarm Reminders:**
    - Set alarms on your phone with playful affirmations. When the alarm sounds, take a moment to repeat the affirmation and infuse positivity into your routine.
    - **Playful Affirmation Wall Art:**
    - Design playful affirmation wall art with colorful and vibrant messages. Decorate your living space with this personalized artwork to uplift your spirits.
    - **Affirmation Exchange with Friends:**
    - Share playful affirmations with friends and create an affirmation exchange. Exchange affirmations regularly to support each other's positive mindset.
    - **Playful Affirmation Cards:**
    - Craft playful affirmation cards with different affirmations written on them. Draw a card randomly each day and let the affirmation guide your positive thoughts.
21. **Laughter Yoga at Work:**
    - **Laughter Yoga Breaks:**
    - Incorporate laughter yoga breaks during work hours. Schedule short breaks where employees can engage in laughter yoga exercises to rejuvenate their energy and reduce stress.
    - **Laughter Yoga Challenges:**
    - Initiate laughter yoga challenges among colleagues. Encourage friendly competition by setting goals for the number of laughter minutes achieved collectively, fostering camaraderie.
    - **Laughter Yoga Team-building Events:**
    - Arrange team-building events centered around laughter yoga. These events promote teamwork, enhance communication, and create a positive and cohesive work environment.
    - **Laughter Yoga Icebreaker Sessions:**
    - Begin meetings or workshops with laughter yoga icebreaker sessions. This sets a positive tone, reduces tension, and creates a relaxed atmosphere for effective communication.
    - **Laughter Yoga Leadership Sessions:**
    - Provide laughter yoga sessions specifically designed for leadership teams. This encourages leaders to model positivity, improve team dynamics, and inspire a healthy work culture.
22. **Playful Water Activities:**
    - Incorporate playfulness into water activities, enjoying the lightness and freedom that water brings, whether it's swimming or water balloon fights.
23. **Humorous Podcasts:**
    - Subscribe to humorous podcasts for a dose of laughter during daily commutes or leisure time.
24. **Playful Cooking Sessions:**
    - Turn cooking into a playful experience, experimenting with new recipes or hosting a fun cooking competition with friends.
25. **Laughter Treasure Hunt:**
    - Organize a laughter treasure hunt, where participants follow clues and engage in laughter-inducing activities at each stop.

Part Eight:
Lifestyle Adjustments

Time Management
for the Overwhelmed

1. **Prioritization Techniques:**
   - Implement the Eisenhower Matrix, categorizing tasks into urgent, important, less important, and non-urgent to prioritize effectively.
   - Utilize the "Eat That Frog" method, tackling the most challenging task first to build momentum.

2. **Time Blocking:**
   - **Theme-Based Time Blocking:**
   - Assign specific themes to different days or blocks of time. For example, dedicate one day to creative work, another to meetings, and a separate block for administrative tasks.
   - **Priority-Based Time Blocks:**
   - Within each time block, prioritize tasks based on importance. Focus on high-priority items first to ensure critical work is completed during the designated time.
   - **Flexibility within Blocks:**
   - Allow flexibility within time blocks to accommodate unexpected tasks or changes in priorities. This adaptive approach prevents stress when unexpected issues arise.
   - **Buffer Time:**
   - Integrate buffer periods between time blocks to account for potential delays or overruns in tasks.
   - **Review and Adjust:**
   - Regularly review the effectiveness of your time blocks. Assess whether tasks were completed within the allocated time and make adjustments as needed.
   - **Batch Similar Tasks:**
   - Enhance efficiency by grouping similar tasks within a time block. For instance, handle all email correspondence or administrative duties during a specific block.
   - **Limit Meeting Times:**
   - Designate specific blocks for meetings to avoid interruptions throughout the day. Set clear start and end times for meetings to ensure they stay within the allocated period.

3. **Setting SMART Goals:**
   - Establish Specific, Measurable, Achievable, Relevant, and Time-bound goals to provide clarity and focus.
   - Break down larger goals into smaller, manageable tasks for a sense of accomplishment.

4. **Batch Processing:**
   - Group similar tasks together and address them during dedicated time periods. This minimizes context-switching, enhancing overall efficiency.
   - Apply this technique to activities like responding to emails or handling administrative tasks.

5. **Time Audits:**
   - **Time Log Analysis:**
   - Maintain a detailed time log for a week or more, documenting how you spend each hour. Analyze the log to identify patterns, time sinks, and opportunities for improvement.
   - **Identify Productivity Peaks:**
   - Assess your time log to pinpoint periods when your productivity is at its peak. Schedule critical or challenging tasks during these high-energy periods for optimal results.
   - **Eliminate Time Wasters:**
   - Identify and eliminate activities that consistently consume time without significant value. This could include excessive social media use, prolonged meetings, or unnecessary tasks.
   - **Delegate Non-Essential Tasks:**
   - Review your time log to identify tasks that can be delegated. Delegating non-essential responsibilities frees up your time for more strategic or high-impact activities.
   - **Batch Processing for Efficiency:**

- Group similar tasks together during specific time blocks to capitalize on the efficiency gained from focused, repetitive work. This reduces context-switching and enhances overall productivity.
  - **Evaluate Distractions:**
- Identify common sources of distractions during your work hours. Implement strategies to minimize or eliminate these distractions, whether they come from colleagues, devices, or environmental factors.

6. **Mindful Time Management:**
   - Practice mindfulness to stay present in the current task, avoiding distractions and promoting a more focused work environment.

7. **Delegate and Outsource:**
   - Delegate tasks that others can handle, freeing up your time for higher-priority activities.
   - Explore outsourcing options for tasks that fall outside your expertise or consume too much time.

8. **Effective Communication:**
   - Clearly communicate deadlines and expectations to team members or collaborators to avoid last-minute rushes.
   - Foster open communication to address challenges and prevent misunderstandings.

9. **Learn to Say No:**
   - **Clarify Your Priorities:**
   - Clearly define your priorities and values. This clarity makes it easier to discern whether a new commitment aligns with your overarching goals and whether saying "yes" contributes positively to your life.
   - **Establish Personal and Professional Boundaries:**
   - Set clear boundaries for both personal and professional life. Clearly communicate these boundaries to others to manage expectations regarding your availability and commitment.
   - **Practice Assertiveness:**
   - Develop assertiveness in expressing your limits. Communicate your capacity and politely decline additional tasks when necessary. This empowers you to maintain control over your time and energy.
   - **Consider Your Current Workload:**
   - Before accepting new commitments, assess your current workload. Understanding your existing responsibilities helps you make informed decisions about taking on additional tasks.
   - **Learn the Art of Diplomatic Declination:**
   - Cultivate diplomatic ways to decline requests. Express gratitude for the opportunity but clearly state that you're unable to take on additional responsibilities at the moment.

10. **Technology Use:**
    - Leverage productivity tools and apps to streamline tasks, manage schedules, and set reminders.
    - Explore time-tracking apps to gain insights into your usage patterns and make informed adjustments.

11. **Regular Breaks:**
    - **Microbreaks for Mental Refreshment:**
    - Implement microbreaks throughout your day, consisting of short, one to two-minute pauses. These quick breaks provide mental refreshment without disrupting your workflow.
    - **Mindful Breathing Breaks:**
    - Integrate mindful breathing exercises during breaks. Focus on deep, intentional breaths to center yourself and alleviate tension. This simple practice can enhance relaxation and mental clarity.
    - **Change of Environment:**
    - Use breaks as an opportunity for a change of environment. Step outside for fresh air, move to a different room, or take a brief walk to break the monotony and stimulate your mind.
    - **Digital Detox Breaks:**
    - Consider incorporating digital detox breaks, where you disconnect from screens. Use this time to engage in non-digital activities like reading a physical book or enjoying nature to reduce eye strain and mental fatigue.

- **Hydration Breaks:**
- Schedule breaks for hydration. Staying adequately hydrated is crucial for cognitive function and overall health. Take short breaks to drink water or herbal tea, promoting both physical and mental well-being.
- **Social Connection Breaks:**
- Use breaks to foster social connections. Connect with colleagues, friends, or family members during your downtime. Social interactions contribute to emotional well-being and can provide a positive mental boost.
- **Creative Expression Breaks:**
- Incorporate breaks for creative expression. Engage in activities like doodling, sketching, or writing for a few minutes. Creative expression can serve as a mental outlet and enhance overall well-being.
- **Expressive Movement Breaks:**
- Integrate expressive movement breaks into your routine. Dance, stretch, or practice yoga during breaks to release physical tension and stimulate circulation, contributing to both physical and mental vitality.

12. **Goal Setting with Deadlines:**
- Set clear deadlines for each task or goal to create a sense of urgency.
- Break down larger projects into smaller, time-bound milestones to track progress.

13. **Continuous Learning:**
- **Online Courses and Workshops:**
- Explore online courses and workshops focused on time management and productivity. Platforms like Coursera, Udemy, or LinkedIn Learning offer a variety of resources to enhance your skills.
- **Time Management Webinars:**
- Attend webinars and virtual sessions dedicated to time management. These live events often provide insights from experts and allow for interactive learning and Q&A sessions.
- **Reading Time Management Books:**
- Allocate time for reading books on time management. Authors like David Allen, Stephen Covey, and Brian Tracy have written extensively on the subject, offering valuable insights and practical tips.
- **Podcasts on Productivity:**
- Incorporate podcasts into your routine that focus on productivity and time management. Podcasts are a convenient way to absorb information while commuting or during breaks.
- **Time Management Apps and Tools:**
- Explore and familiarize yourself with new time management apps and tools. Stay informed about the latest technologies that can streamline your workflow and improve time utilization.

14. **Self-Care Practices:**
- Prioritize self-care to maintain overall well-being, as a healthy mind and body contribute to better time management.
- Ensure sufficient sleep, exercise, and relaxation to boost productivity during work hours.

15. **Reflection and Adjustment:**
- Regularly reflect on your time management strategies, identifying what works and what needs adjustment.
- Be flexible and willing to refine your approach based on evolving priorities and circumstances.

The Importance of
Leisure and Downtime

1. 1. **Definition of Leisure:**
    *   Understand that leisure refers to voluntary activities pursued for pleasure and relaxation. It involves choosing activities that bring joy and contribute to a sense of well-being.
2. **Distinguishing Leisure from Work:**
    *   **Create a Designated Workspace:**
    *   Designate a specific area for work-related activities. Having a dedicated workspace helps in physically separating work from leisure, fostering a clear boundary.
    *   **Set Fixed Work Hours:**
    *   Establish fixed work hours to create a structured routine. Clearly define when your workday begins and ends, allowing for a clear transition into leisure time.
    *   **Define Work Goals and Limits:**
    *   Clearly define daily or weekly work goals and limits.
        Knowing what needs to be accomplished during work hours helps prevent the encroachment of tasks into leisure time.
    *   **Use Tools for Time Management:**
    *   Utilize time management tools or techniques, such as the Pomodoro Technique or time blocking, to enhance productivity during work hours. This ensures focused work, leaving ample time for leisure.
    *   **Power Down Work Devices:**
    *   Power down work-related devices at the end of the workday. This action signifies the end of the work shift and prevents the temptation to check emails or engage in work tasks during leisure hours.
    *   **Create Rituals for Transition:**
    *   Establish rituals to mark the transition from work to leisure. This could include a brief walk, a specific activity, or a mindfulness exercise that signifies the end of work responsibilities.
3. **Benefits of Downtime:**
    *   Recognize the essential benefits of downtime, including mental and physical rejuvenation. Downtime allows the mind to rest, recharge, and return to tasks with increased focus and creativity.
4. **Stress Reduction through Leisure:**
    *   Engage in leisure activities as a proactive approach to stress reduction. Pursuing enjoyable and non-work-related activities helps counteract the negative effects of stress, contributing to overall well-being.
5. **Types of Leisure Activities:**
    *   **Hobbies for Creativity:**
    *   Engage in hobbies that spark creativity, such as painting, drawing, writing, or crafting. Creative pursuits offer a therapeutic outlet and stimulate the imagination.
    *   **Outdoor Recreation:**
    *   Embrace outdoor leisure activities like hiking, biking, or picnics. Spending time in nature provides a refreshing change of scenery and promotes physical well-being.
    *   **Mindful Meditation:**
    *   Incorporate mindful meditation into your leisure routine. Practices like mindfulness or guided meditation can calm the mind and alleviate stress.
    *   **Cultural Exploration:**
    *   Explore cultural leisure activities such as visiting museums, attending concerts, or experiencing local events. Immersing yourself in cultural pursuits adds richness to your leisure time.

- **Reading for Relaxation:**
- Dive into reading as a leisure activity. Whether it's fiction, non-fiction, or poetry, reading allows for mental escape and provides a gateway to different worlds.
- **Cooking and Culinary Adventures:**
- Experiment with cooking or baking as a leisurely pursuit. Trying out new recipes or cuisines can be both enjoyable and rewarding.

6. **Balancing Active and Passive Leisure:**
   - Strike a balance between active and passive leisure. Active activities, like hiking or playing sports, provide physical engagement, while passive activities, like reading or listening to music, offer relaxation without physical exertion.

7. **Mindful Leisure Engagement:**
   - Practice mindfulness during leisure activities.
   Be fully present in the moment, savoring the experience without distractions. Mindful engagement enhances the enjoyment and relaxation derived from leisure.

8. **Scheduled Leisure Time:**
   - Intentionally schedule leisure time into your routine. Treat it with the same importance as work commitments, ensuring that you allocate dedicated periods for activities that bring you joy and relaxation.

9. **Setting Leisure Goals:**
   - Set goals for leisure activities. Whether it's finishing a novel, mastering a new recipe, or achieving a fitness milestone, having goals enhances the sense of accomplishment and fulfillment in leisure pursuits.

10. **Digital Detox during Leisure:**
    - **Mindful Unplugging:**
    - Practice mindful unplugging during leisure by consciously turning off notifications and silencing electronic devices. This allows you to focus on the present moment and fully engage in your chosen leisure activity.
    - **Designate Device-Free Zones:**
    - Establish specific areas in your home or specific activities during which electronic devices are not allowed. This creates designated spaces for genuine leisure without digital distractions.
    - **Screen-Free Outdoor Activities:**
    - Opt for screen-free outdoor leisure activities. Whether it's a nature walk, gardening, or a picnic, immersing yourself in the outdoors without screens enhances the experience and promotes relaxation.
    - **Analog Hobbies:**
    - Embrace analog hobbies that don't involve electronic devices. Engage in activities like drawing, reading physical books, or playing musical instruments for a tech-free leisure experience.
    - **Socializing Without Screens:**
    - Prioritize face-to-face interactions during leisure time. Whether it's meeting friends for coffee, playing board games, or having a picnic, socializing without screens fosters genuine connections.
    - **Digital Decluttering:**
    - Dedicate leisure time to digital decluttering. Organize and clean up your digital space, including emails, files, and apps. A streamlined digital environment can contribute to a sense of order and calm.

11. **Socializing in Leisure:**
    - Incorporate socializing into leisure activities. Spending time with friends or family during leisure contributes to social well-being, fostering connections and emotional support.

12. **Exploration of New Hobbies:**
    - Periodically explore new hobbies or leisure pursuits. Trying new activities not only adds excitement but also introduces variety, preventing monotony and enhancing the overall leisure experience.

13. **Personalized Leisure Preferences:**
    - Understand and honor your personalized leisure preferences. Recognize that what brings relaxation and joy varies for each individual, and tailor your leisure choices to align with your unique preferences.

14. **Leisure as Self-Care:**
    - View leisure as a form of self-care. It is a vital component of maintaining mental health and preventing burnout. Prioritize leisure as an investment in your overall well-being.
15. **Reflective Leisure:**
    - Incorporate reflective leisure activities. Whether it's journaling, meditation, or quiet contemplation, reflective leisure provides a space for introspection and self-discovery.
16. **Creating Leisure Rituals:**
    - Establish leisure rituals, such as a weekly movie night, a nature walk on weekends, or a monthly art session. Rituals add predictability and structure to leisure, enhancing the anticipation and enjoyment of these activities.
17. **Unstructured Downtime:**
    - Allow for unstructured downtime. Not every moment needs to be filled with planned activities. Allowing for spontaneous and unstructured downtime provides flexibility for rest and relaxation.
18. **Incorporating Leisure into Travel:**
    - Integrate leisure into travel plans. While exploring new destinations, include activities that align with your leisure preferences. Travel can be an enriching opportunity to experience diverse leisure pursuits.
19. **Leisure for Stress Recovery:**
    - Acknowledge that leisure serves as a powerful tool for stress recovery. When facing challenges or intense periods of work, deliberately increase leisure time to support resilience and prevent burnout.
20. **Setting Boundaries for Leisure:**
    - Establish boundaries to protect your leisure time. Communicate with others about the importance of these periods, ensuring that you have uninterrupted and quality moments for relaxation.
21. **Leisure for Personal Growth:**
    - Embrace the potential for personal growth through leisure. Engaging in activities that challenge or inspire you contributes to continuous learning and self-improvement.
22. **Mindful Leisure Transition:**
    - Practice mindful transitions between work and leisure.
    Allow a brief period to shift your mindset, leaving work-related thoughts behind before immersing yourself in leisure activities.
23. **Expressive Leisure Outlets:**
    - Consider expressive leisure outlets, such as art, writing, or music. These activities provide a channel for self-expression and emotional release, adding depth to your leisure experiences.
24. **Leisure as a Social Connector:**
    - Utilize leisure as a social connector. Join clubs, classes, or groups centered around your leisure interests to foster connections with like-minded individuals.
25. **Regular Evaluation of Leisure Choices:**
    - Regularly evaluate your leisure choices. Ensure that the activities you engage in continue to bring joy and relaxation, adjusting your leisure repertoire as your preferences evolve.

Cultivating a Hobby:
Joyful Expressions

1. **Self-Exploration:**
   - Begin by exploring your interests and passions. Reflect on activities that bring you joy and fulfillment. This self-discovery process is crucial for finding a hobby that resonates with you.
2. **Start Small:**
   - **Exploratory Phase:**
   - Treat the initial stages as an exploratory phase. Experiment with diverse activities, even those outside your comfort zone. This phase is about discovering what resonates with you on a personal level.
   - **Curiosity as a Guide:**
   - Let curiosity be your guide. Follow your interests and inclinations without imposing rigid expectations. Allow the journey of exploration to unfold organically.
   - **Sampling Different Activities:**
   - Sample a variety of activities within a short period. This could include trying out a new instrument, attempting a simple art project, or exploring outdoor activities.
   - **Temporary Commitments:**
   - Make temporary commitments to various activities. Rather than investing heavily upfront, commit to trying something for a defined period. This approach minimizes pressure and allows for flexibility.
   - **Reflective Journaling:**
   - Maintain a reflective journal during the exploratory phase. Document your feelings, preferences, and experiences with each activity. This journal can serve as a valuable tool for self-discovery.
   - **Identifying Preferences:**
   - Pay attention to activities that naturally capture your interest. Identifying preferences involves noticing the moments when you feel most engaged, fulfilled, or excited during different hobbies.
3. **Mindful Engagement:**
   - Approach your chosen hobby with mindfulness. Fully immerse yourself in the present moment while engaging in the activity. This mindful engagement enhances the therapeutic benefits of the hobby.
4. **Set Realistic Goals:**
   - Establish realistic and achievable goals related to your hobby. Setting milestones provides a sense of accomplishment and motivation, contributing to a positive and rewarding experience.
5. **Create a Dedicated Space:**
   - Designate a specific space for your hobby. Whether it's a corner of a room, a garden shed, or a studio space, having a dedicated area enhances focus and allows for a seamless transition into your hobby.
6. **Variety in Hobbies:**
   - Consider exploring a variety of hobbies to keep things interesting. Having multiple hobbies caters to different aspects of your personality and provides a well-rounded approach to joyful expressions.
7. **Social Hobbies:**
   - **Community Classes and Workshops:**
   - Enroll in community classes or workshops related to your chosen hobby. These structured environments provide opportunities to meet and connect with individuals who share similar interests.
   - **Online Forums and Communities:**
   - Join online forums and communities dedicated to your hobby. Platforms such as social media groups or specialized forums allow you to interact with enthusiasts from around the world, expanding your social circle.

- **Attend Meetup Events:**
- Explore Meetup events centered around your hobby. Meetup is a platform that facilitates in-person gatherings, offering a chance to connect with local hobbyists and build meaningful relationships.
- **Organize Hobby Nights:**
- Host or participate in hobby nights with friends or community members. These gatherings can include activities, discussions, or collaborative projects related to your shared interests.
- **Participate in Group Projects:**
- Collaborate on group projects within your hobby community. This fosters a sense of camaraderie and allows you to contribute your skills while learning from others.
- **Create a Hobby Club:**
- Establish a hobby club with friends or acquaintances who share similar interests. This provides a dedicated space for regular interactions, discussions, and joint activities related to your chosen hobby.

8. **Embrace Creativity:**
   - Cultivate hobbies that allow for creative expression. Whether it's painting, writing, or crafting, engaging in creative pursuits enhances self-expression and contributes to a sense of joy.
9. **Learn Continuously:**
   - Embrace a mindset of continuous learning within your hobby. Attend workshops, read books, or watch tutorials to enhance your skills and knowledge. The learning process adds depth to your hobby.
10. **Adaptability in Hobbies:**
    - Choose hobbies that offer flexibility and adaptability. This allows you to tailor your hobby to your schedule and preferences, preventing it from becoming a source of stress.
11. **Mindful Crafting:**
    - If your hobby involves crafting, practice mindfulness in the creative process. Pay attention to the details, textures, and colors. This meditative approach enhances the therapeutic aspects of crafting.
12. **Regular Practice:**
    - Dedicate regular time to practice your hobby. Consistency fosters improvement, and the routine of engaging in joyful activities contributes positively to your overall well-being.
13. **Explore New Techniques:**
    - Keep your hobby dynamic by exploring new techniques or styles. This prevents monotony and introduces fresh challenges, stimulating creativity and enthusiasm.
14. **Mindful Photography:**
    - If photography is your hobby, practice mindful photography. Pay attention to the composition, lighting, and subject. This not only improves your photography skills but also enhances the experience.
15. **Document Your Journey:**
    - Keep a journal or create a blog to document your journey in your hobby.
    Reflecting on your progress, challenges, and achievements adds a reflective and introspective dimension to your joyful expressions.
16. **Incorporate Music:**
    - Integrate music into your hobby routine. Whether you're painting, gardening, or crafting, playing music enhances the atmosphere and contributes to an overall enjoyable experience.
17. **Therapeutic Gardening:**
    - If gardening is your hobby, approach it with a therapeutic mindset. Pay attention to the sensory aspects of gardening, from the feel of soil to the fragrance of flowers. This mindful approach elevates the experience.
18. **Joyful Culinary Adventures:**
    - Explore joyful culinary adventures as a hobby. Experiment with new recipes, ingredients, and cooking techniques. Cooking and baking can be both a creative and satisfying endeavor.
19. **Celebrate Milestones:**
    - **Organize Achievement Showcases:**

- Host showcases or exhibitions to display the work of individuals who have achieved significant milestones. This collective celebration not only recognizes individual accomplishments but also inspires others within the hobby community.
- **Virtual Milestone Celebrations:**
- Arrange virtual milestone celebrations where participants can share their achievements through video calls or online platforms. This fosters a sense of connection and collective joy, even in a digital environment.
- **Create Milestone Badges:**
- Design and distribute virtual or physical badges that hobbyists can earn upon reaching specific milestones. This tangible recognition adds a fun and rewarding aspect to the journey, motivating individuals to strive for new heights.
- **Collaborative Milestone Projects:**
- Initiate collaborative projects or challenges that align with achieving milestones.
  This encourages participants to set personal goals and contribute collectively to a larger endeavor, fostering a sense of community accomplishment.

20. **Nature-Inspired Art:**
    - If your hobby involves art, draw inspiration from nature. Create art that reflects the beauty and serenity of the natural world. This connection with nature enhances the therapeutic aspects of your hobby.

21. **Mindful Writing:**
    - If writing is your hobby, practice mindful writing. Allow your thoughts to flow freely, and focus on the process rather than the end result. This form of self-expression can be cathartic and fulfilling.

22. **Integrate Fitness:**
    - Choose hobbies that incorporate physical activity. Whether it's dancing, hiking, or yoga, the combination of joyful expression and movement contributes to both physical and mental well-being.

23. **Experiment with DIY Projects:**
    - Engage in do-it-yourself (DIY) projects as a hobby. From home decor to personalized gifts, the process of creating something with your hands can be immensely satisfying.

24. **Reflect and Learn:**
    - Periodically reflect on your hobby experience. Identify aspects that bring you the most joy and consider how you can enhance those elements. Learning from your experiences contributes to a more fulfilling hobby.

25. **Share Your Passion:**
    - Share your hobby with others. Whether through teaching, showcasing your creations, or simply discussing your interests, sharing your passion creates a positive ripple effect and enhances the overall enjoyment of your hobby.

Digital Detox:
Unplugging to Unwind

1. **Establishing Tech-Free Zones:**
   - Designate specific areas in your home, such as the bedroom or dining area, as tech-free zones. This creates spaces where you can unwind without the constant presence of digital devices.
2. **Scheduled Device Breaks:**
   - **Micro-Breaks for Eye Health:**
   - Incorporate micro-breaks every 20-30 minutes, especially if you engage in prolonged screen time. During these breaks, focus on activities like looking at distant objects to reduce eye strain and prevent digital eye fatigue.
   - **Mindful Breathing Breaks:**
   - Use device breaks as opportunities for mindful breathing exercises. Step away from your screen, close your eyes, and take a few deep breaths. This brief pause can enhance mental clarity and reduce stress.
   - **Nature Breaks:**
   - Step outside during device breaks and immerse yourself in nature, whether it's a short walk in the park or just spending a few minutes in your garden. Fresh air and natural surroundings can have a rejuvenating effect on your mind.
   - **Stretching and Movement Breaks:**
   - Integrate light stretching or movement exercises into your device breaks. Simple stretches or a quick walk around your workspace can alleviate physical tension and boost energy levels.
   - **Social Interaction Breaks:**
   - Use breaks as opportunities for brief social interactions, either in person or virtually. Connecting with a colleague, friend, or family member during these breaks fosters social bonds and provides a mental refresh.
3. **Notification Management:**
   - Customize notification settings to minimize disruptions. Turn off non-essential notifications during focused work or leisure time to reduce the constant influx of digital stimuli.
4. **Mindful Social Media Use:**
   - Practice mindful and intentional use of social media. Set specific time limits for social media engagement and curate your feed to include content that uplifts and inspires rather than induces stress.
5. **Digital Sabbath:**
   - Designate one day a week as a "digital Sabbath" where you completely disconnect from electronic devices. This intentional break allows for genuine relaxation and fosters a deeper connection with the non-digital aspects of life.
6. **Unplugged Activities:**
   - Engage in activities that don't involve screens, such as reading a physical book, practicing a hobby, or spending time in nature. Diversifying activities contributes to a more balanced and fulfilling lifestyle.
7. **Technology-Free Mealtime:**
   - Make mealtimes technology-free zones. Focus on savoring your food and engaging in meaningful conversations without the distraction of screens.
8. **Digital Sunset Ritual:**
   - Create a "digital sunset" ritual where you gradually reduce screen time as the evening progresses.
   This prepares your mind for a restful night's sleep by minimizing exposure to blue light before bedtime.
9. **Offline Hobbies:**
   - Cultivate offline hobbies that allow you to express creativity or engage in physical activities. Whether it's painting, gardening, or playing a musical instrument, these pursuits offer a break from digital demands.

10. **Mindful Digital Consumption:**
    - Practice mindful consumption of digital content. Before diving into online activities, ask yourself if they align with your well-being goals, and be intentional about the content you choose to engage with.
11. **Tech-Free Retreats:**
    - Plan occasional tech-free retreats or vacations. Disconnecting from the digital world during getaways provides a chance to recharge, connect with surroundings, and fully immerse yourself in the present moment.
12. **Digital Decluttering:**
    - Regularly declutter your digital space by organizing files, deleting unused apps, and unsubscribing from unnecessary emails.
    A clean digital environment contributes to a sense of order and reduces digital stressors.
13. **No-Tech Morning Routine:**
    - Begin your day without immediately reaching for digital devices. Establish a morning routine that includes activities like meditation, stretching, or enjoying a leisurely breakfast before diving into the digital realm.
14. **Analog Journaling:**
    - Embrace analog journaling as a way to reflect, plan, and express thoughts without the use of digital tools. The tactile experience of writing on paper can be therapeutic and grounding.
15. **Digital Accountability Partners:**
    - **Set Clear Boundaries:**
    - Establish clear boundaries with your accountability partner regarding the specifics of your digital detox. Clearly define what activities are off-limits and communicate expectations to ensure a shared understanding.
    - **Regular Check-Ins:**
    - Schedule regular check-in sessions with your accountability partner.
    These sessions can provide an opportunity to discuss challenges, share successes, and offer encouragement to stay on track with the digital detox plan.
    - **Celebrate Milestones Together:**
    - Celebrate milestones and achievements together. Whether it's completing a designated period of reduced screen time or overcoming a specific digital dependency, acknowledging successes reinforces the positive impact of the digital detox journey.
    - **Share Strategies and Tips:**
    - Exchange strategies and tips for managing digital use. Your accountability partner may have insights or techniques that prove effective, contributing to a collaborative and supportive approach to the digital detox process.
    - **Create Joint Activities:**
    - Plan and engage in joint activities that do not involve digital devices. This could include outdoor outings, board games, or shared hobbies, fostering a strong connection while reducing reliance on screens.
16. **Offline Self-Care Practices:**
    - Incorporate offline self-care practices, such as meditation, deep breathing exercises, or a warm bath, to unwind without the reliance on digital resources.
17. **Tech-Free Sleep Environment:**
    - Create a tech-free zone in your bedroom to improve sleep quality. Remove electronic devices, including smartphones and tablets, to minimize disturbances and promote a more restful night's sleep.
18. **Digital Detox Challenges:**
    - **Themed Detox Challenges:**
    - Design digital detox challenges with specific themes. For example, focus on reducing social media usage during one challenge and limiting overall screen time in another. Themed challenges add variety and address different aspects of digital dependency.
    - **Gradual Time Reduction:**
    - Implement challenges that involve gradual time reduction. Start with a week-long challenge and progressively extend it to longer durations. This incremental approach helps individuals acclimate to reduced screen time without feeling overwhelmed.

- **Device-Specific Challenges:**
- Create challenges that target specific devices. For instance, dedicate a challenge to minimizing smartphone usage, followed by challenges for other devices like tablets or computers. This allows for a more focused approach to reducing dependence on each digital platform.
- **Social Detox Challenges:**
- Explore challenges centered around social interactions. During these challenges, prioritize face-to-face conversations, phone calls, or handwritten notes over digital communication. This not only reduces screen time but also enhances interpersonal connections.
- **Offline Activity Bingo:**
- Develop an "Offline Activity Bingo" challenge. Create a bingo card with various offline activities, and participants aim to complete a line or full card within a specified timeframe. This gamified approach adds an element of fun and exploration to the digital detox journey.

19. **Tech-Free Mindfulness Sessions:**
   - Attend in-person or virtual mindfulness sessions that specifically promote a tech-free environment.
   These sessions can guide you through relaxation techniques and mindfulness practices without the distraction of screens.

20. **Create a Digital-Free Hour:**
   - Dedicate one hour each day to being completely digital-free.
   Use this time for activities that bring joy, relaxation, or personal growth without the influence of digital devices.

21. **Offline Learning Opportunities:**
   - Explore offline learning opportunities, such as attending workshops, classes, or community events. Engaging in face-to-face learning experiences enhances personal connections and reduces screen dependency.

22. **Digital-Free Travel Experiences:**
   - Plan travel experiences where you intentionally disconnect from digital devices. Immerse yourself in the local culture, scenery, and activities without the constant need for online connectivity.

23. **Mindful Digital Reintroduction:**
   - When returning to digital activities after a break, do so mindfully.
   Assess how each digital interaction contributes to your well-being, and be intentional about reintegrating technology into your routine.

24. **Tech-Free Outdoor Adventures:**
   - Embark on outdoor adventures without the reliance on technology. Whether it's hiking, camping, or simply enjoying a day at the beach, nature provides a rejuvenating backdrop for tech-free experiences.

25. **Reflect on Digital Detox Benefits:**
   - Regularly reflect on the positive effects of digital detox in your life. Acknowledge improvements in sleep, mood, and overall well-being as motivation to maintain a balanced relationship with technology.

Part Nine:
Coping Strategies

Mindful Coping During Unexpected Events

1. Mindful Awareness of the Present Moment:
- Begin by cultivating mindfulness, an awareness of the present moment. Practice observing thoughts and feelings without judgment. This foundation allows for a more centered and composed response to unexpected events.

2. Grounding Techniques:
- **Mindful Observation:**
- Practice mindful observation by paying close attention to your surroundings. Notice the colors, shapes, and textures around you. This sensory awareness helps bring your focus to the present moment.
- **Five Senses Exercise:**
- Engage your five senses deliberately. Identify five things you can see, four things you can touch, three things you can hear, two things you can smell, and one thing you can taste. This sensory exploration grounds you in the current experience.
- **Body Scan Meditation:**
- Perform a body scan meditation, systematically bringing awareness to each part of your body. This helps release tension and fosters a connection between your mind and body.
- **Grounding Objects:**
- Keep small objects with you that have significance or soothing textures. Holding onto these objects during unexpected events provides a physical anchor, creating a sense of familiarity and comfort.
- **Mindful Breathing with Counting:**
- Practice mindful breathing while counting your breaths. Inhale deeply, counting to a specific number, and then exhale slowly, maintaining the count. This rhythmic breathing aids in grounding and relaxation.
- **Visualization Techniques:**
- Use visualization to create a mental anchor. Picture a place or scenario that brings you calmness and security. Imagining this setting during unexpected events can provide a mental refuge.
- **Mantra Repetition:**
- Repeat a comforting mantra or affirmation.
  Choose a phrase that resonates with you, and repeat it silently or aloud. This verbal grounding technique can shift your focus and promote a sense of stability.

3. Acceptance of the Unpredictable:
- Embrace the concept of impermanence and unpredictability. Acknowledge that unexpected events are a natural part of life, and acceptance can lead to a more balanced and less reactive mindset.

4. Non-Attachment to Outcomes:
- Practice non-attachment to specific outcomes. While it's natural to have preferences, being overly attached to a particular result can lead to stress. Embrace flexibility and openness to alternative possibilities.

5. Mindful Decision-Making:
- **Pause and Reflect:**
- Cultivate the habit of pausing before making decisions. This brief moment of reflection allows you to step back from automatic reactions and approach the decision with greater awareness.
- **Clarify Your Values:**
- Before making a decision, clarify your values. Consider what truly matters to you in the given situation. Aligning your choices with your core values promotes a sense of authenticity and fulfillment.

- **Mindful Breathing:**
- Integrate mindful breathing into the decision-making process. Take a few deep breaths to center yourself and bring focus to the present moment. This practice helps calm the mind and enhances clarity.
- **Consider Long-Term Impacts:**
- Mindful decision-making involves considering the long-term impacts of your choices. Assess how a decision aligns with your overarching goals and aspirations, fostering a forward-thinking perspective.
- **Non-Judgmental Awareness:**
- Approach the decision-making process with non-judgmental awareness. Instead of labeling options as good or bad, observe them objectively. This mindset reduces unnecessary stress and allows for a more balanced evaluation.
- **Embrace Uncertainty:**
- Recognize and embrace the inherent uncertainty in decision-making.
  Mindfulness encourages a more flexible mindset, enabling you to adapt to unexpected outcomes and learn from experiences.
- **Body Awareness:**
- Connect with your body's sensations during decision-making. Notice any tension, discomfort, or ease. This awareness of bodily cues can provide valuable insights into your intuitive responses.

6. Cultivating Resilience:
- Develop resilience through mindfulness. Resilience involves bouncing back from adversity. Regular mindfulness practice strengthens the ability to adapt to unexpected events and navigate challenges with greater ease.

7. Compassionate Self-Talk:
- **Identify Negative Self-Talk:**
- Start by identifying negative or self-critical thoughts that may arise during unexpected events. Awareness is the first step toward transforming negative self-talk into a more compassionate and constructive dialogue.
- **Challenge Unhelpful Thoughts:**
- Challenge unhelpful thoughts by questioning their validity. Ask yourself if these thoughts are based on facts or if they are influenced by emotional reactions. This critical examination helps you gain perspective.
- **Replace with Positive Affirmations:**
- Replace negative thoughts with positive affirmations. Cultivate a list of affirmations that resonate with you and counteract self-criticism. Repeat these affirmations to yourself during challenging moments.
- **Embrace a Growth Mindset:**
- Adopt a growth mindset by viewing challenges as opportunities for learning and growth. Instead of seeing unexpected events as failures, consider them as valuable experiences that contribute to your personal development.
- **Cultivate Self-Compassion:**
- Cultivate self-compassion by acknowledging that everyone faces challenges and makes mistakes. Treat yourself with the same kindness you would offer a friend in difficult circumstances.

8. Mindful Responses vs. Reactions:
- Differentiate between reactions and responses.
  Reactions are often impulsive and driven by emotions, while responses are thoughtful and considerate. Mindfulness provides the space to choose a response rather than react impulsively.

9. Release of Control:
- Acknowledge the limits of control. While it's natural to desire control over situations, many aspects of life are beyond our control. Mindful coping involves releasing unnecessary attachments to control and embracing the fluidity of life.

10. Mindful Movement in Stressful Times:
- Integrate mindful movement practices during stressful times. Activities like yoga, tai chi, or walking with awareness can help channel excess energy and promote a sense of calm during unexpected events.

11. Intentional Pauses:
- Incorporate intentional pauses during the day. Brief moments of stillness and reflection can serve as anchors, allowing you to reset and approach unexpected events with a more composed mindset.

12. Mindful Listening:
- Practice mindful listening during challenging conversations.
  Give full attention to the speaker, without formulating responses in your mind. This fosters better understanding and promotes effective communication.

13. Gratitude Practice:
- Cultivate a gratitude practice. Even in the midst of unexpected events, identifying elements for which you are grateful can shift your perspective and contribute to a more positive outlook.

14. Mindful Eating Habits:
- Extend mindfulness to eating habits during stressful times. Pay attention to the flavors, textures, and sensations of each bite. Mindful eating can be a grounding practice amid uncertainty.

15. Journaling for Reflection:
- Engage in reflective journaling. Write down your thoughts and feelings about unexpected events. This process enhances self-awareness and provides an outlet for processing emotions.

16. Setting Mindful Intentions:
- Set mindful intentions for your day. Before facing unexpected events, establish clear intentions about how you want to respond. This proactive approach aligns actions with values.

17. Mindful Breathing Techniques:
- Incorporate various mindful breathing techniques.
  Whether it's diaphragmatic breathing, box breathing, or alternate nostril breathing, these techniques can promote relaxation and resilience during unexpected events.

18. Mindfulness-Based Stress Reduction (MBSR):
- Explore structured programs like Mindfulness-Based Stress Reduction (MBSR). These programs offer systematic training in mindfulness, equipping individuals with tools to cope with stress and navigate challenges more effectively.

19. Mindful Visualization:
- Utilize mindful visualization techniques. Envision positive outcomes or visualize yourself navigating unexpected events with calmness and resilience. Visualization can influence your mindset and responses.

20. Mindful Sleep Practices:
- Implement mindful sleep practices. Ensure a restful sleep environment, practice relaxation techniques before bedtime, and approach sleep with a mindful awareness of the body and breath.

21. Mindful Detox from Information:
- Detox from constant information consumption. Be mindful of the media and information you expose yourself to during unexpected events. Taking breaks from excessive news or social media can prevent overwhelm.

22. Mindful Time Management:
- Approach time management mindfully. Break down tasks into manageable steps, prioritize, and allocate time intentionally. Mindful time management reduces stress related to overwhelming workloads.

23. Mindful Communication in Relationships:
- Apply mindfulness to communication within relationships. Ensure that your words are thoughtful and considerate, fostering open and constructive dialogue, especially during challenging times.

Long-Term Strategies vs. Short-Term Relief

Long-Term Strategies: Building Resilience for Sustainable Well-Being

1. **Holistic Wellness Approach:**
   - Develop a holistic approach to wellness, encompassing physical, mental, and emotional dimensions. Focus on long-term lifestyle choices that contribute to overall well-being.

2. **Mindful Nutrition:**
   - **Nutrient-Rich Choices:**
   - Prioritize nutrient-dense foods, such as fruits, vegetables, whole grains, lean proteins, and healthy fats. These choices provide essential vitamins, minerals, and antioxidants for overall health.
   - **Hydration Habits:**
   - Cultivate a habit of staying hydrated by drinking an adequate amount of water throughout the day. Hydration is crucial for various bodily functions, including cognitive performance and stress regulation.
   - **Balanced Macronutrients:**
   - Maintain a balance of carbohydrates, proteins, and fats in your meals. Each macronutrient plays a unique role in energy provision, satiety, and overall well-being.
   - **Mindful Eating Practices:**
   - Practice mindful eating by paying attention to the sensory experience of each meal. Chew slowly, savor flavors, and be present during meals, fostering a healthier relationship with food.
   - **Portion Control:**
   - Be mindful of portion sizes to avoid overeating. Understanding appropriate portions helps regulate calorie intake and supports weight management.
   - **Regular Meal Timing:**
   - Establish regular meal timings to maintain stable blood sugar levels. Consistent meal schedules contribute to sustained energy levels and help prevent energy crashes.
   - **Limit Processed Foods:**
   - Reduce the intake of highly processed and refined foods. Opt for whole, minimally processed options to maximize nutritional benefits and minimize added sugars and unhealthy fats.

3. **Regular Exercise Routine:**
   - Establish a consistent exercise routine that aligns with personal preferences and health goals. Regular physical activity contributes not only to physical fitness but also to stress resilience.

4. **Cultivating Mindfulness:**
   - Integrate mindfulness practices, such as meditation and mindful breathing, into daily life. Cultivating mindfulness over time enhances awareness, reduces reactivity to stressors, and fosters mental resilience.

5. **Continuous Learning and Growth:**
   - Embrace a mindset of continuous learning and personal growth. Engaging in ongoing education, acquiring new skills, and pursuing intellectual challenges contribute to a sense of purpose and fulfillment.

6. **Building Supportive Relationships:**
   - Invest time and effort in building and nurturing supportive relationships. Long-term emotional connections provide a reliable foundation for coping with stress and life challenges.

7. **Effective Time Management:**
   - Develop effective time management skills to prioritize tasks, set realistic goals, and maintain a healthy work-life balance. Long-term success in time management contributes to reduced stress.

8. **Financial Planning:**
   - **Goal Setting:**
   - Establish clear financial goals, both short-term and long-term. Whether it's saving for a major purchase, building an emergency fund, or planning for retirement, defined goals provide direction and purpose to your financial planning.
   - **Budgeting Practices:**
   - Develop a realistic budget that outlines income, expenses, and savings. Categorize expenditures to understand where money is allocated, allowing for informed decisions and identifying areas for potential savings.
   - **Emergency Fund Creation:**
   - Prioritize the creation of an emergency fund to cover unforeseen expenses. Having a financial safety net provides peace of mind and helps mitigate stress during unexpected financial challenges.
   - **Debt Management:**
   - Implement a strategy for managing and reducing debt. Prioritize high-interest debts and explore consolidation options to streamline payments and potentially reduce interest rates.
   - **Regular Financial Check-ins:**
   - Schedule regular check-ins to review your financial situation. This proactive approach enables you to track progress, adjust goals as needed, and identify potential issues before they become major concerns.
   - **Professional Financial Advice:**
   - Consider seeking advice from a certified financial planner or advisor. Professionals can offer personalized insights, strategies, and investment guidance tailored to your specific financial circumstances and goals.
9. **Emotional Intelligence Development:**
   - Work on enhancing emotional intelligence. Developing self-awareness, self-regulation, empathy, and interpersonal skills contributes to better stress management and healthier relationships.
10. **Establishing Healthy Boundaries:**
   - Establish and maintain healthy boundaries in personal and professional life. Clear boundaries prevent burnout and foster a sustainable balance between responsibilities.

Short-Term Relief Techniques: Immediate Strategies for Stress Reduction
1. **Deep Breathing Exercises:**
   - Practice deep breathing exercises for instant stress relief. Deep, intentional breaths activate the body's relaxation response and provide a quick way to calm the nervous system.
2. **Progressive Muscle Relaxation (PMR):**
   - Engage in PMR, a technique involving tensing and relaxing different muscle groups. This short-term strategy helps release physical tension and promotes a state of relaxation.
3. **Mindful Pause:**
   - **Micro-Mindful Pauses:**
   - Integrate micro-mindful pauses into your routine, even if only for a minute or two. These brief breaks allow for a reset and can be done anywhere, whether at your desk, in a meeting, or while commuting.
   - **Mindful Breathing Techniques:**
   - Practice mindful breathing exercises during pauses. Focus on your breath, inhaling and exhaling slowly and intentionally. This simple technique helps calm the nervous system and promotes a sense of centeredness.
   - **Observing Surroundings:**
   - Use mindful pauses to observe your surroundings. Take a moment to notice the colors, textures, and sounds in your environment. Engaging your senses in this way fosters a connection with the present moment.
4. **Laughter Therapy:**
   - Incorporate laughter into the day. Whether through humor, watching a funny video, or engaging in light-hearted activities, laughter triggers the release of endorphins, providing a quick mood boost.

5. **Gratitude Practice:**
   - Practice gratitude during moments of stress. Reflecting on positive aspects of life in the present moment can shift focus and provide immediate relief from negative emotions.
6. **Quick Physical Activity:**
   - Engage in short bursts of physical activity. A quick walk, a set of stretches, or a brief workout can release tension and boost energy levels in the short term.
7. **Visualization Exercises:**
   - Use visualization exercises for mental escapism. Guided imagery or picturing calming scenes can provide a brief respite from stressors.
8. **Mindful Eating Moments:**
   - Practice mindful eating during stressful times. Focusing on the sensory experience of eating, even for a few moments, can break the cycle of stress-related overeating.
9. **Expressive Writing:**
   - Engage in expressive writing as a quick emotional release. Taking a few minutes to jot down thoughts and feelings can provide immediate relief during stressful situations.
10. **Aromatherapy Breaks:**
    - Incorporate aromatherapy breaks. Inhaling calming scents like lavender or chamomile can trigger a relaxation response and offer a quick reprieve.

Harmonizing Long-Term Strategies and Short-Term Relief
- **Recognizing Individual Needs:**
  - Understand that individuals have unique preferences and needs. What works as a long-term strategy for one person may differ for another. Tailor approaches to personal preferences.
- **Creating a Toolkit:**
  - Develop a personalized toolkit that combines long-term strategies and short-term relief techniques. Having a range of tools allows for flexibility in addressing stress at different levels.
- **Regular Reflection and Adjustment:**
  - Periodically reflect on the effectiveness of strategies and techniques. Adjust the approach as needed to accommodate changes in lifestyle, priorities, or individual circumstances.
- **Integrating Mindfulness into Daily Life:**
  - **Mindful Breathing Moments:**
  - Incorporate short mindful breathing moments throughout the day. Take a few conscious breaths during transitions, such as moving from one task to another or entering a new environment.
  - **Mindful Eating Practices:**
  - Practice mindful eating during meals. Pay attention to the flavors, textures, and sensations of each bite. This not only enhances your dining experience but also promotes a healthy relationship with food.
  - **Mindful Commuting:**
  - Use commuting time as an opportunity for mindfulness. Whether walking, driving, or using public transport, be present in the moment. Notice the sights, sounds, and sensations of your journey.
  - **Mindful Technology Use:**
  - Be mindful of your technology use. Instead of mindlessly scrolling through social media, set intentional periods for device use. This fosters a conscious approach to technology and reduces information overload.
  - **Mindful Listening Practices:**
  - Practice mindful listening in conversations. Give your full attention to the speaker, avoid formulating responses while they talk, and truly engage in understanding their perspective.

Chapter 3

Handling Work-Related Stress

1. **Prioritization and Time Management:**
   - **Time Blocking:**
   - Implement time blocking, where you allocate specific blocks of time for different activities. This structured approach helps create a visual representation of your day and enhances focus on individual tasks.
   - **Task Sequencing:**
   - Sequence tasks logically based on dependencies and energy levels. Tackle more demanding or creative tasks during your peak hours and reserve less intensive activities for other times.
   - **Weekly Planning Sessions:**
   - Conduct weekly planning sessions to map out tasks and goals for the upcoming week. This proactive approach helps in anticipating workload and strategizing accordingly.
2. **Effective Goal Setting:**
   - Set clear, achievable goals for yourself. Break down larger tasks into smaller, manageable steps, creating a sense of accomplishment as you progress.
3. **Communication and Boundaries:**
   - Communicate effectively with colleagues and superiors. Clearly express your workload and set realistic boundaries to manage expectations. Learn to say no when necessary.
4. **Mindful Work Breaks:**
   - Take short breaks during the workday to reset your mind. Engage in brief mindfulness exercises, deep breathing, or a short walk to relieve stress and enhance focus.
5. **Positive Affirmations at Work:**
   - **Morning Affirmation Ritual:**
   - Begin your workday with a set of positive affirmations. This ritual can set a constructive tone, fostering optimism and mental resilience for the tasks ahead.
   - **Tailor Affirmations to Specific Goals:**
   - Customize affirmations to align with specific work-related goals. Whether it's completing a project, leading a team, or overcoming obstacles, tailor affirmations to reinforce your commitment to success.
   - **Team Affirmations:**
   - Introduce team affirmations during collaborative meetings. Encourage team members to share positive affirmations related to teamwork, innovation, and achieving collective objectives.
6. **Task Delegation:**
   - Delegate tasks when possible. Recognize that you don't have to carry the entire workload alone. Trusting others with responsibilities can alleviate stress and foster a collaborative work environment.
7. **Workspace Organization:**
   - Maintain an organized workspace. Clutter can contribute to feelings of overwhelm. Keep your work area tidy and create a conducive environment for productivity.
8. **Constructive Feedback and Recognition:**
   - Seek constructive feedback and recognize your achievements. A healthy feedback loop can help you refine your skills, while acknowledging your accomplishments boosts motivation.
9. **Regular Check-Ins:**
   - Schedule regular check-ins with your supervisor or team. These meetings provide an opportunity to discuss progress, challenges, and potential adjustments to workload or expectations.
10. **Flexible Work Arrangements:**
    - Explore flexible work arrangements if possible. Negotiate options such as remote work or flexible hours to create a work environment that aligns with your preferences and reduces stress.

11. **Task Batching:**
    - Batch similar tasks together to maximize efficiency.
    Grouping similar activities allows you to focus on one type of work at a time, reducing the cognitive load associated with constant context-switching.

12. **Mindful Transition from Work to Home:**
    - Establish a mindful transition from work to home. Create a ritual or routine that signifies the end of the workday, allowing you to mentally disconnect and shift your focus to personal life.

13. **Conflict Resolution Skills:**
    - Develop effective conflict resolution skills. Address workplace conflicts promptly and constructively, seeking solutions that benefit all parties involved.

14. **Self-Care at Work:**
    - Integrate self-care practices into your workday.
    This can include short meditation sessions, stretching exercises, or moments of mindfulness to refresh your mind and body.

15. **Professional Development Opportunities:**
    - Pursue professional development opportunities. Continuous learning and skill enhancement can boost your confidence and make work-related challenges more manageable.

16. **Healthy Snack Choices:**
    - Make mindful choices when it comes to snacks. Opt for nutritious options that support sustained energy levels throughout the day, preventing energy crashes.

17. **Effective Email Management:**
    - Manage your email effectively. Set specific times to check and respond to emails, reducing the constant influx of messages that can contribute to stress.

18. **Expressing Gratitude at Work:**
    - Practice gratitude in the workplace. Acknowledge the efforts of your colleagues, express appreciation for teamwork, and foster a positive and supportive work culture.

19. **Continuous Learning Mindset:**
    - Cultivate a continuous learning mindset. Embrace challenges as opportunities for growth, viewing setbacks as lessons that contribute to your professional development.

20. **Mindful Lunch Breaks:**
    - Take mindful lunch breaks. Step away from your work area, eat mindfully, and use this time to recharge. Avoid working through lunch, allowing your mind to rest.

21. **Effective Meeting Strategies:**
    - Optimize meeting efficiency. Set clear agendas, establish goals for each meeting, and encourage active participation. Efficient meetings contribute to a more streamlined work experience.

22. **Creative Problem-Solving:**
    - Approach challenges with creative problem-solving techniques. Consider alternative solutions, think outside the box, and collaborate with colleagues to find innovative approaches to work-related issues.

23. **Stress-Reduction Techniques:**
    - Incorporate stress-reduction techniques into your routine. This can include progressive muscle relaxation, guided imagery, or other practices that help manage stress levels.

24. **Regular Physical Activity:**
    - Integrate regular physical activity into your routine. Exercise is a powerful stress reducer, releasing endorphins that contribute to a positive mood and improved resilience.

25. **Establishing Work-Life Balance:**
    - Strive for a healthy work-life balance. Set boundaries to prevent work from encroaching into personal time, allowing for relaxation, family, and other fulfilling activities outside of work.

Stress Management for Parents and Caregivers

1. **Effective Time Management:**
   - Prioritize tasks and create a realistic schedule. Allocate time for both caregiving responsibilities and personal activities to avoid feeling overwhelmed.
2. **Establishing a Support System:**
   - **Online Parenting Communities:**
   - Join online parenting communities or forums where you can connect with other parents facing similar challenges. Share experiences, seek advice, and offer support in a virtual space.
   - **Local Parenting Groups:**
   - Explore local parenting groups or meet-ups where you can interact with parents in your community. This provides an opportunity for face-to-face connections and the sharing of local resources.
   - **Parenting Workshops and Classes:**
   - Attend parenting workshops or classes in your area. These forums not only provide valuable information but also serve as a platform for meeting other parents who are invested in their personal growth.
   - **Professional Support Services:**
   - Consider seeking support from professionals such as therapists, counselors, or family coaches. These individuals can provide guidance on parenting strategies and coping mechanisms tailored to your specific situation.
   - **Extended Family Involvement:**
   - If possible, involve extended family members in caregiving responsibilities. Grandparents, aunts, uncles, or other relatives can share the load, providing much-needed breaks for primary caregivers.
3. **Setting Realistic Expectations:**
   - Understand that perfection is unattainable. Set realistic expectations for yourself as a parent and caregiver, recognizing that it's okay to ask for help or seek support when needed.
4. **Practicing Self-Compassion:**
   - Be kind to yourself. Parenting comes with challenges, and it's essential to practice self-compassion. Acknowledge your efforts and forgive yourself for any perceived shortcomings.
5. **Effective Communication with Partners:**
   - Maintain open and honest communication with your partner. Share responsibilities and discuss challenges to ensure you are on the same page, working together as a team.
6. **Mindful Parenting Practices:**
   - Embrace mindfulness in parenting. Be fully present with your child during interactions, fostering a deeper connection and reducing stress associated with distraction.
7. **Self-Care Rituals:**
   - Carve out time for self-care. Whether it's a short break, a hobby, or simply some quiet time, prioritizing self-care contributes to emotional well-being.
8. **Balancing Work and Family Life:**
   - **Effective Time Blocking:**
   - Implement time-blocking techniques to allocate specific periods for work, family, and personal activities.
   - Use visual aids like calendars to create a clear schedule that promotes a balance between work and family commitments.
   - **Prioritize Self-Care:**
   - Recognize the importance of self-care in maintaining overall well-being.
   - Schedule regular self-care activities, such as exercise, relaxation, or hobbies, to recharge and better handle both work and family responsibilities.
   - **Open Communication:**
   - Foster open communication with family members about work demands and commitments.

- Set realistic expectations and discuss how to support each other in maintaining a balanced family life.
- **Flexibility in Work Arrangements:**
- If possible, explore flexible work arrangements that accommodate family needs.
- Negotiate options such as telecommuting or flexible hours to strike a balance between professional and family responsibilities.

9. **Effective Delegation of Tasks:**
   - Delegate tasks when possible. Whether it's involving children in age-appropriate chores or seeking help from others, effective delegation lightens the overall workload.

10. **Creating a Flexible Routine:**
    - Develop a flexible routine that accommodates unexpected events. Flexibility helps reduce stress when plans deviate from the expected.

11. **Mindful Breathing Exercises:**
    - Practice mindful breathing to manage stress in the moment. Take slow, deep breaths to calm the nervous system and regain composure.

12. **Embracing Imperfections:**
    - Understand that imperfections are a natural part of parenting. Embrace the messiness of parenthood and focus on the joyous moments rather than striving for perfection.

13. **Regular Family Meetings:**
    - Conduct regular family meetings to discuss schedules, address concerns, and foster open communication. This ensures everyone feels heard and understood.

14. **Utilizing Parenting Resources:**
    - Explore available parenting resources, such as books, online forums, or support groups. Learning from others' experiences can provide valuable insights and coping strategies.

15. **Mindful Decision-Making:**
    - Approach parenting decisions mindfully. Take the time to assess situations, consider different perspectives, and make choices that align with your family values.

16. **Strengthening Emotional Bonds:**
    - **Self-Care Rituals:**
    - Establish self-care rituals that fit into your daily routine. These could include short breaks, moments of relaxation, or engaging in activities you enjoy to recharge.
    - **Time Management for Parents:**
    - Implement effective time management strategies, such as creating schedules and routines, to balance work, parenting responsibilities, and personal time.
    - **Quality Family Time:**
    - Prioritize quality over quantity when spending time with your family. Engage in activities that foster connection and create meaningful memories.
    - **Delegating Responsibilities:**
    - Learn to delegate tasks and responsibilities, both at work and at home. Delegating helps distribute the workload and prevents the accumulation of stressors.

17. **Building a Routine for Children:**
    - Establish a consistent routine for children. Predictability and structure can create a sense of security for both parents and children.

18. **Gratitude Practices:**
    - **Gratitude Journaling:**
    - Keep a gratitude journal where you regularly jot down things you're thankful for in your parenting journey. This practice encourages a positive outlook and helps you appreciate the small, meaningful moments.
    - **Daily Gratitude Rituals:**
    - Establish daily rituals that involve expressing gratitude. This could be sharing moments of gratitude during family meals or bedtime, creating a positive and appreciative atmosphere at home.
    - **Gratitude Letters or Notes:**
    - Write letters or notes of gratitude to your children, partner, or other family members. This not only communicates your appreciation but also strengthens emotional connections within the family.

- **Gratitude Collages:**
- Create visual representations of gratitude through collages or vision boards. Include pictures, drawings, or words that symbolize aspects of parenting that bring you joy and fulfillment.
- **Family Gratitude Jar:**
- Introduce a family gratitude jar where each family member can contribute notes expressing gratitude. Take turns reading these notes during designated family times.
- **Gratitude Walks with Children:**
- Incorporate gratitude into outdoor activities. During nature walks or outings, encourage your children to express gratitude for the environment, experiences, or each other.
- **Mindful Gratitude Moments:**
- Integrate mindful moments of gratitude into daily routines. This could be taking a few minutes during diaper changes, meal preparation, or bedtime to reflect on the positive aspects of parenting.

19. **Socializing with Other Parents:**
     - Engage with other parents to share experiences and offer mutual support. Social connections with fellow parents provide a sense of community.
20. **Conflict Resolution Skills:**
     - Develop effective conflict resolution skills within the family. Teach children healthy ways to express themselves, fostering a harmonious home environment.
21. **Mindful Eating Habits:**
     - Pay attention to eating habits. Provide nutritious meals for both yourself and your children, as proper nutrition plays a role in overall well-being.
22. **Quality Sleep for Parents:**
     - Prioritize quality sleep. Establish a bedtime routine for yourself to ensure adequate rest, promoting emotional resilience.
23. **Celebrating Achievements:**
     - Celebrate milestones and achievements, both big and small. Recognizing and celebrating successes contributes to a positive family atmosphere.
24. **Encouraging Independence in Children:**
     - Foster independence in children by encouraging age-appropriate responsibilities. This not only eases the parental load but also promotes children's self-confidence.
25. **Creating Relaxing Family Time:**
     - Designate specific times for relaxing family activities. Whether it's movie nights, nature walks, or simple games, shared enjoyable experiences contribute to family bonding and stress reduction.

Part Ten:
Inner Peace and Spirituality

Finding Your Path
to Inner Peace

1. **Mindfulness Meditation:**
   - Cultivate a mindfulness meditation practice. This involves focusing on the present moment, observing thoughts without judgment, and fostering a sense of inner calm.
2. **Breathing Techniques:**
   - **Mindfulness Meditation:**
   - Practice mindfulness meditation to bring your attention to the present moment. Focus on your breath, sensations, and thoughts without judgment.
   - **Mind-Body Practices:**
   - Explore mind-body practices such as tai chi, qigong, or yoga. These activities integrate movement, breath, and mindfulness to enhance overall well-being.
   - **Nature Connection:**
   - Spend time in nature to connect with the soothing elements of the outdoors. Nature walks, hiking, or simply sitting in a peaceful environment can contribute to inner peace.
   - **Gratitude Journaling:**
   - Keep a gratitude journal to reflect on and appreciate positive aspects of your life. Cultivating gratitude fosters a positive mindset and inner calm.
   - **Silent Retreats:**
   - Consider participating in silent retreats to disconnect from external noise and immerse yourself in a serene and contemplative environment.
   - **Digital Detox Days:**
   - Designate specific days for a digital detox, minimizing screen time and allowing your mind to disengage from the constant influx of information.
   - **Reading Inspirational Literature:**
   - Explore literature that inspires and uplifts. Books, poems, or quotes that resonate with your values and aspirations can be powerful tools for finding inner peace.
   - **Mindful Breathing Techniques:**
   - Practice mindful breathing techniques, such as box breathing or 4-7-8 breathing, to regulate your breath and induce a state of calmness.
3. **Mindful Awareness of Thoughts:**
   - Develop mindful awareness of your thoughts. Notice negative or intrusive thoughts without attaching to them, allowing them to pass without causing undue stress.
4. **Journaling for Reflection:**
   - **Expressive Writing:**
   - Engage in expressive writing by allowing your thoughts and feelings to flow freely onto paper. This unstructured form of writing can be a cathartic and illuminating process.
   - **Gratitude Journaling:**
   - Dedicate a section of your journal to gratitude. Regularly noting down things you're grateful for can shift your focus toward positive aspects of your life, fostering a sense of appreciation.
   - **Goal Setting and Progress Tracking:**
   - Use your journal to set personal and professional goals. Track your progress, celebrate achievements, and reassess goals over time. This structured approach provides a roadmap for personal development.
   - **Emotional Release:**
   - Journaling serves as a safe space to release pent-up emotions. Write about challenging experiences, frustrations, or joys to process and validate your emotions.
   - **Morning Pages:**
   - Adopt the practice of "morning pages," where you write three pages of stream-of-consciousness thoughts as soon as you wake up. This ritual can clear your mind and set a positive tone for the day.

- **Problem Solving:**
- Use your journal to work through problems or challenges. Write about potential solutions, analyze pros and cons, and gain clarity on your decision-making process.
- **Dream Journaling:**
- Keep a dream journal to record your dreams upon waking. Dreams can offer insights into your subconscious and provide a creative outlet for self-discovery.
- **Self-Reflection Prompts:**
- Utilize self-reflection prompts to guide your journaling sessions.
  Questions like "What am I grateful for today?" or "What would I like to improve about myself?" can stimulate deeper introspection.

5. **Visualization and Guided Imagery:**
   - Practice visualization or guided imagery exercises. Envision peaceful scenes or scenarios that evoke feelings of tranquility, helping to create a mental space for inner peace.

6. **Yoga and Tai Chi for Mind-Body Connection:**
   - Engage in mind-body practices like yoga or Tai Chi. These disciplines combine physical movement with breath awareness, fostering a deeper connection between the body and mind.

7. **Silent Retreats:**
   - **Mindful Walking Retreats:**
   - Participate in silent walking retreats, where the focus is on mindfully moving through natural surroundings. This combines the benefits of meditation with physical activity.
   - **Artistic Silent Retreats:**
   - Explore silent retreats that incorporate artistic expression, such as painting, drawing, or sculpting.
     Engaging in creative activities without verbal communication can deepen the introspective experience.
   - **Digital Detox Silent Retreats:**
   - Opt for silent retreats that encourage a complete digital detox. Disconnecting from electronic devices allows for a more profound connection with the self and the surrounding environment.
   - **Nature Immersion Silent Retreats:**
   - Choose silent retreats set in natural settings like mountains, forests, or by the ocean. The serenity of nature enhances the contemplative atmosphere.
   - **Mindful Eating Retreats:**
   - Experience silent retreats that incorporate mindful eating practices. Paying full attention to the sensory experience of eating fosters a deeper connection with food.

8. **Nature Immersion:**
   - Spend time in nature to reconnect with the natural world. Whether it's a walk in the park, a hike, or simply sitting in a garden, nature has a calming influence on the mind.

9. **Digital Detox Weekends:**
   - Plan occasional digital detox weekends. Disconnect from electronic devices to reduce external stimuli and create a space for inner peace and reflection.

10. **Mindful Listening Practices:**
    - Practice mindful listening in your interactions with others. Fully engage in conversations, giving your complete attention and fostering a deeper connection.

11. **Gratitude and Positive Affirmations:**
    - **Gratitude Journaling:**
    - Establish a daily gratitude journal where you record three things you're grateful for. Reflecting on positive aspects of your life fosters a sense of appreciation.
    - **Expressing Gratitude to Others:**
    - Make it a habit to express gratitude to people in your life. Write thank-you notes or simply convey your appreciation verbally. This not only benefits them but enhances your own sense of well-being.
    - **Gratitude Walks:**
    - Incorporate gratitude into your walks. As you stroll, focus your thoughts on things you're grateful for, whether it's the beauty of nature or positive aspects of your life.
    - **Morning Gratitude Ritual:**
    - Begin your day with a gratitude ritual. Before getting out of bed, take a moment to reflect on things you're thankful for. This sets a positive tone for the day ahead.

- **Gratitude Jar:**
- Create a gratitude jar where you deposit notes about things you're grateful for. Over time, revisit these notes to remind yourself of the positive elements in your life.
- **Gratitude Meditation:**
- Integrate gratitude meditation into your mindfulness practice. Focus your meditation on feelings of gratitude, allowing them to permeate your thoughts and emotions.
- **Gratitude Board:**
- Develop a visual gratitude board. Use pictures, quotes, or notes to represent the things you're thankful for. Place it in a prominent spot as a daily reminder.

12. **Artistic Expression:**
    - Explore artistic expression as a means of self-discovery and relaxation. Whether through painting, writing, or other creative outlets, expressing yourself artistically can be therapeutic.

13. **Reading Inspirational Literature:**
    - Read inspirational literature or philosophical texts that resonate with your values and beliefs. Thought-provoking content can provide insights and contribute to inner peace.

14. **Mindful Eating Practices:**
    - Practice mindful eating by savoring each bite and being fully present during meals. This fosters a connection between your mind and body and promotes a sense of peace.

15. **Cultivating Compassion:**
    - **Loving-Kindness Meditation:**
    - Practice loving-kindness meditation to enhance compassion. Direct well-wishes and positive intentions towards yourself, loved ones, acquaintances, and even those you may find challenging.
    - **Random Acts of Kindness:**
    - Engage in random acts of kindness as a way to express compassion. Small gestures, whether for strangers or friends, contribute to a more compassionate and interconnected world.
    - **Self-Compassion Practices:**
    - Develop self-compassion through mindful self-talk and acknowledging imperfections. Treat yourself with the same kindness and understanding you would offer a friend facing difficulties.
    - **Empathy Building Exercises:**
    - Participate in exercises that enhance empathy. This could involve reading literature from different perspectives, attending empathy workshops, or engaging in role-playing scenarios.
    - **Compassion for Nature:**
    - Extend compassion to the natural world. Acknowledge the interconnectedness of all living beings and practice environmentally conscious behaviors as an expression of care.
    - **Compassion and Conflict Resolution:**
    - Apply compassion to conflict resolution. Approach disagreements with empathy, seeking to understand the perspectives of others and finding common ground for resolution.

The Role of Spirituality
in Relieving Stress

1. **Mindful Meditation Practices:**
   - Engage in mindfulness meditation rooted in spiritual traditions. Focus on the present moment, your breath, or a mantra, allowing stress to dissipate as you cultivate inner peace.
2. **Prayer and Contemplation:**
   - Incorporate prayer or contemplative practices into your daily routine. Connecting with a higher power or the divine can provide a sense of solace and guidance during stressful times.
3. **Spiritual Breathing Techniques:**
   - **Box Breathing with Spiritual Affirmations:**
   - Practice box breathing, a technique involving inhaling, holding, exhaling, and holding the breath in equal counts. Infuse this practice with spiritual affirmations, reinforcing a sense of calm and connection.
   - **Pranayama Techniques:**
   - Explore pranayama, the ancient yogic practice of breath control.
     Incorporate specific pranayama techniques, such as Nadi Shodhana (alternate nostril breathing) or Kapalabhati (skull-shining breath), with a focus on spiritual intention.
   - **Guided Spiritual Visualization with Breath:**
   - Combine guided spiritual visualization with breathwork. Inhale positive energy and exhale stress, visualizing your breath as a conduit for spiritual light and renewal.
   - **Breath of Fire Meditation:**
   - Engage in the Breath of Fire meditation, a rapid and rhythmic breath pattern from Kundalini Yoga. Align this practice with spiritual aspirations, using the breath to awaken inner energy and vitality.
   - **Chanting Mantras with Breath:**
   - Integrate chanting mantras with breath awareness. As you inhale and exhale, synchronize the rhythm with the repetition of a spiritually significant mantra, fostering a meditative and tranquil state.
4. **Mindful Walking in Nature:**
   - Practice mindful walking in natural surroundings.
     Allow the beauty of nature to be a backdrop for your spiritual connection, fostering a sense of tranquility and stress relief.
5. **Sacred Rituals and Traditions:**
   - Embrace sacred rituals and traditions from your spiritual background. Whether it's lighting candles, chanting, or participating in religious ceremonies, these practices can instill a sense of calm.
6. **Guided Spiritual Visualizations:**
   - Engage in guided spiritual visualizations. Picture a serene, spiritually significant place in your mind, immersing yourself in the tranquility of that mental space.
7. **Spiritual Affirmations:**
   - Create and recite spiritual affirmations. Affirm your connection to higher principles, emphasizing qualities like love, compassion, and resilience as you navigate life's challenges.
8. **Journaling for Spiritual Reflection:**
   - Maintain a spiritual journal for reflection. Write about your spiritual journey, experiences, and insights gained during moments of stress, fostering a deeper connection with your spirituality.
9. **Mindful Eating Practices:**
   - Integrate mindful eating practices with a spiritual focus. Offer gratitude for your meals, savoring each bite as a sacred experience, promoting a mindful and stress-reducing approach to nourishment.

10. **Spiritual Music and Chants:**
    - Listen to spiritual music or chants. The rhythmic patterns and meaningful lyrics can evoke a sense of peace, providing an auditory anchor for stress relief.
11. **Silent Retreats:**
    - Attend silent retreats with a spiritual focus. These retreats offer dedicated time for introspection, prayer, and communion with your spiritual beliefs.
12. **Connection to Spiritual Community:**
    - **Participate in Spiritual Gatherings:**
    - Attend regular spiritual gatherings, whether they are in-person or virtual. Engaging in group rituals, ceremonies, or discussions fosters a sense of unity and shared purpose.
    - **Join Spiritual Study Groups:**
    - Become a member of a spiritual study group focused on exploring sacred texts, teachings, or philosophical discussions. This intellectual engagement within a community can deepen your understanding and connection.
    - **Collaborate on Service Projects:**
    - Volunteer for service projects organized by your spiritual community. Collaborating on initiatives that contribute to the well-being of others creates a shared sense of purpose and fulfillment.
    - **Participate in Retreats:**
    - Attend spiritual retreats organized by your community. Retreats offer dedicated time for reflection, meditation, and communal experiences, strengthening the bonds among participants.
    - **Contribute to Community Events:**
    - Play an active role in organizing or contributing to community events. Whether it's a celebration, festival, or educational program, your involvement enhances the communal spirit.
    - **Create Online Discussion Forums:**
    - Establish online discussion forums or social media groups for your spiritual community. These platforms provide a space for continuous interaction, sharing insights, and supporting each other.
13. **Spiritual Study and Reflection:**
    - Engage in the study of spiritual texts and reflective practices. Extract wisdom from sacred scriptures or teachings, applying them to your life for guidance during stressful periods.
14. **Mindful Yoga Practices:**
    - Practice mindful yoga with a spiritual foundation. Connect each movement with a deeper spiritual intention, fostering a holistic approach to stress relief through body and spirit.
15. **Digital Detox for Spiritual Reconnection:**
    - Implement a digital detox with a focus on spiritual reconnection. Temporarily disconnect from technology to create sacred, uninterrupted moments for spiritual practices.
16. **Spiritual Retreats in Nature:**
    - Attend spiritual retreats held in natural settings. The combination of spiritual practices and immersion in nature can amplify the stress-relieving benefits.
17. **Compassion and Forgiveness Practices:**
    - **Self-Compassion Meditation:**
    - Engage in meditation practices that specifically focus on cultivating self-compassion. This involves acknowledging your own struggles, mistakes, and imperfections with a gentle and understanding mindset.
    - **Loving-Kindness Meditation:**
    - Incorporate loving-kindness meditation into your spiritual routine. This practice involves directing positive intentions and well-wishes not only towards yourself but also towards others, fostering a compassionate outlook.
    - **Gratitude as a Path to Compassion:**
    - Cultivate gratitude as a means of nurturing compassion. Regularly express gratitude for the positive aspects of your life, fostering a mindset that appreciates and acknowledges the good in yourself and others.

- **Mindful Compassion in Daily Interactions:**
- Practice mindful compassion in your daily interactions. Pay attention to the needs and emotions of others, responding with empathy and kindness, thus contributing to a more harmonious environment.
- **Generosity and Acts of Kindness:**
- Integrate acts of kindness and generosity into your routine. Small gestures, whether towards yourself or others, can have a profound impact on fostering a compassionate mindset.
- **Compassionate Communication:**
- Adopt compassionate communication techniques. This involves expressing yourself honestly while being mindful of the feelings and perspectives of others, creating an atmosphere of understanding and empathy.

18. **Connection to Sacred Symbols:**
   - Establish a connection to sacred symbols. Whether through religious symbols or spiritually significant imagery, having a visual representation can serve as a focal point for stress relief.

19. **Spiritual Mindfulness Apps:**
   - Utilize mindfulness apps with a spiritual focus. These apps often provide guided meditations, affirmations, and practices aligned with various spiritual traditions.

20. **Integration of Spirituality into Daily Life:**
   - Infuse spirituality into your daily life. Intentionally align your actions and decisions with your spiritual beliefs, creating a harmonious and stress-reducing lifestyle.

21. **Spiritual Mentorship:**
   - Seek guidance from a spiritual mentor or teacher. Having a mentor can provide support, insights, and a deeper understanding of your spiritual path, aiding in stress management.

22. **Fasting or Cleansing Rituals:**
   - Explore fasting or cleansing rituals with a spiritual context. Many spiritual traditions incorporate periods of fasting, which can offer both physical and spiritual benefits.

23. **Spiritual Mind-Body Practices:**
   - Engage in mind-body practices rooted in spirituality. Tai Chi, Qi Gong, or other disciplines can promote physical well-being while nurturing spiritual connection and stress relief.

24. **Connection to Sacred Texts:**
   - Read and reflect on sacred texts. Extract wisdom from spiritual literature that resonates with your beliefs, applying the teachings to find solace in challenging moments.

25. **Integration of Gratitude into Spirituality:**
   - Integrate gratitude practices into your spiritual routine. Expressing gratitude for spiritual blessings and life's gifts can shift your focus away from stressors, fostering a positive and balanced mindset.

Meditation Practices
for Everyday Calm

1. **Mindful Breathing Meditation:**
   - Begin with mindful breathing exercises. Find a quiet space, sit comfortably, and focus your attention on your breath. Inhale deeply, exhale slowly, and observe the sensations of each breath. This simple practice anchors you in the present moment, promoting calmness.

2. **Body Scan Meditation:**
   - **Focused Breath Awareness:**
   - Begin the body scan meditation with focused breath awareness. Take a few deep breaths to center yourself and bring attention to the present moment. This establishes a foundation for the practice.
   - **Toe-to-Head Progression:**
   - Systematically progress from your toes to the top of your head. Direct your attention to each body part, starting with the toes, moving to the feet, ankles, and so on. This sequential approach promotes a thorough and mindful exploration.
   - **Mindful Observation:**
   - As you focus on each body part, practice mindful observation. Notice any sensations, warmth, coolness, or areas of tension. Allow yourself to observe without judgment, cultivating a non-reactive awareness.
   - **Release Tension with Breath:**
   - When you identify areas of tension, consciously breathe into those areas. Inhale deeply, directing the breath to the tense muscles, and exhale, envisioning the tension dissipating. This intentional breathwork enhances the relaxation response.
   - **Progressive Muscle Relaxation (PMR) Integration:**
   - Integrate elements of Progressive Muscle Relaxation (PMR). For tense areas, experiment with tensing the muscles briefly during inhalation and releasing the tension completely during exhalation. This combination enhances the relaxation process.
   - **Visualization for Relaxation:**
   - Incorporate visualization techniques during the body scan. As you focus on each body part, visualize it bathed in a soothing light or surrounded by a sense of warmth. Visualization enhances the mind-body connection and deepens relaxation.
   - **Acknowledging Sensations:**
   - Encourage an open and accepting attitude toward sensations. Whether they are pleasant, neutral, or uncomfortable, acknowledge them without judgment. This acceptance contributes to a sense of inner peace.

3. **Loving-Kindness Meditation:**
   - Integrate loving-kindness meditation into your routine. Cultivate feelings of love and compassion, first towards yourself and then expanding to others. This practice enhances positive emotions and contributes to a more serene state of mind.

4. **Guided Meditation Apps:**
   - Explore guided meditation apps. These apps provide a variety of guided sessions for different purposes, such as stress reduction, sleep, or focus. Follow along with the guidance to enhance your meditation experience.

5. **Visualization Meditation:**
   - Engage in visualization meditation by creating mental images of peaceful scenes or scenarios. Whether it's a serene beach, a calming forest, or a tranquil meadow, visualizing peaceful settings can induce a sense of calm.

6. **Breath Counting Meditation:**
   - **Balanced Breath Cycle:**
   - Maintain a balanced breath cycle. Aim for a comfortable and natural rhythm, avoiding forced or exaggerated breaths. A harmonious breath cycle contributes to a calming and centered meditation experience.
   - **Gentle Inhalation and Exhalation:**
   - Emphasize gentle inhalation and exhalation. Cultivate a soft and effortless breath pattern, allowing the breath to flow naturally. This gentle approach enhances relaxation and minimizes tension.
   - **Counting on the Exhalation:**
   - Experiment with counting only on the exhalation. Sync your counting with the outward flow of breath. This variation encourages a heightened awareness of the breath's release and promotes a serene mental state.
   - **Mindful Body Scan with Breath Counting:**
   - Combine the breath counting meditation with a mindful body scan. As you count each breath, direct your awareness to specific areas of the body.
   - **Breath Counting Variations:**
   - Explore different breath counting variations. You can vary the count, starting from one and gradually increasing to a specific number (e.g., 10) before resetting. Experimenting with variations prevents monotony and engages the mind.
   - **Silent Counting:**
   - Practice silent counting. Instead of audibly counting in your mind, mentally visualize the numbers. Silent counting enhances concentration and minimizes external distractions, creating a more immersive meditative experience.
   - **Rhythmic Breath Counting:**
   - Establish a rhythmic breath counting pattern. Sync the counting with a consistent pace, creating a steady and predictable rhythm. Rhythmic counting supports a tranquil state of mind and enhances the meditative flow.

7. **Mindful Walking Meditation:**
   - Practice mindful walking. Take slow, deliberate steps, paying attention to each movement and the sensations in your feet.
     This form of walking meditation brings awareness to the present moment and can be done indoors or outdoors.

8. **Mantra Meditation:**
   - Utilize mantra meditation by repeating a calming phrase or word. Choose a mantra that resonates with you and recite it silently or aloud. This repetitive focus helps calm the mind and reduce stress.

9. **Transcendental Meditation:**
   - Learn Transcendental Meditation (TM) techniques. This form of meditation involves silently repeating a mantra to reach a state of restful awareness. TM has been associated with reduced stress and enhanced overall well-being.

10. **Metta Meditation:**
    - Practice Metta meditation, also known as compassion meditation. Generate feelings of loving-kindness towards yourself and others. This practice fosters a sense of connection and compassion, promoting emotional balance.

11. **Mindfulness-Based Stress Reduction (MBSR):**
    - Enroll in Mindfulness-Based Stress Reduction programs.
      These structured courses teach mindfulness meditation techniques and their application in daily life for stress reduction and improved mental well-being.

12. **Open Monitoring Meditation:**
    - Engage in open monitoring meditation, where you observe thoughts and sensations without attachment or judgment. This non-reactive awareness cultivates a calm and centered mind.

13. **Silent Meditation Retreats:**
    - Consider participating in silent meditation retreats. These immersive experiences provide an opportunity to deepen your meditation practice in a focused and supportive environment.

14. **Tea Meditation:**
   - Practice tea meditation, a form of mindfulness while preparing and sipping tea. Focus on each step of the process, from boiling water to enjoying each sip mindfully.
15. **Mindful Eating Meditation:**
   - Extend mindfulness to eating. Pay attention to the flavors, textures, and sensations of each bite. Mindful eating promotes a healthier relationship with food and enhances overall well-being.
16. **Morning Meditation Routine:**
   - Establish a morning meditation routine. Starting the day with a few minutes of meditation sets a positive tone and prepares your mind for the challenges and opportunities ahead.
17. **Evening Reflection Meditation:**
   - Conclude the day with an evening reflection meditation. Review the events of the day with a non-judgmental awareness, fostering a sense of closure and relaxation before bedtime.
18. **Breath Awareness Throughout the Day:**
   - Incorporate breath awareness into your daily activities. Take moments throughout the day to focus on your breath, grounding yourself in the present and fostering a calm mindset.
19. **Zen Meditation Practices:**
   - Explore Zen meditation practices. Whether it's Zazen (seated meditation) or Kinhin (walking meditation), Zen techniques emphasize simplicity and direct experience, leading to a tranquil state of mind.
20. **Mindful Tech Usage Meditation:**
   - Integrate mindful tech usage meditation.
   Before engaging with digital devices, take a moment to center yourself through brief meditation, promoting a more intentional and mindful approach to technology.
21. **Progressive Muscle Relaxation (PMR):**
   - Combine meditation with Progressive Muscle Relaxation (PMR). Progressively tense and release different muscle groups while maintaining a mindful awareness, promoting both physical and mental relaxation.
22. **Nature Meditation:**
   - Immerse yourself in nature meditation. Find a peaceful outdoor spot, sit comfortably, and observe the sights, sounds, and sensations around you. Nature meditation enhances connection with the environment and induces a sense of calm.
23. **Mindful Driving Meditation:**
   - Practice mindful driving meditation. Pay full attention to the act of driving, observe your surroundings, and stay present. This approach can turn a daily commute into a mindful and stress-reducing experience.
24. **Visualization for Stress Reduction:**
   - Utilize guided visualization for stress reduction.
   Listen to audio recordings or use your imagination to create mental images that promote relaxation and alleviate stress.
25. **Mindful Transition Meditation:**
   - Incorporate mindful transition meditation between different activities. Take a moment to pause, breathe, and reset your focus before moving from one task to another.

The Healing Nature of Forgiveness and Compassion

1. Self-Reflection:
- Begin by engaging in self-reflection. Understand your emotions, identify areas of resentment or hurt, and acknowledge the impact on your well-being.

2. Mindful Awareness:
- Cultivate mindful awareness of your thoughts and emotions. Practice being present in the moment, observing without judgment, and creating a space for self-compassion.

3. Embrace Empathy:
- **Active Listening:**
- Practice active listening when engaging with the person involved. Give them your full attention, seek to understand their words, and refrain from interrupting. This fosters an open and empathetic communication environment.
- **Ask Open-Ended Questions:**
- Encourage open dialogue by asking open-ended questions about their experiences and feelings.
  This allows for a more comprehensive understanding of their perspective and motivations.
- **Empathetic Body Language:**
- Utilize empathetic body language to convey your openness and understanding. Maintain eye contact, adopt an open posture, and nod affirmatively to signal that you are genuinely engaged in the conversation.
- **Non-Judgmental Attitude:**
- Approach the situation with a non-judgmental attitude. Understand that people make mistakes, and acknowledging their humanity without harsh judgment can contribute to a more empathetic perspective.
- **Expressing Empathy Verbal:**
- Verbally express your empathy. Share statements that convey your understanding of their feelings and experiences. For example, say, "I can imagine that must have been challenging for you."
- **Acknowledge External Factors:**
- Acknowledge external factors that may have influenced their actions. Consider circumstances, stressors, or challenges they were facing, recognizing that external pressures can impact behavior.

- **Reflect on Shared Humanity:**
- Reflect on the shared humanity between you and the person you're forgiving. Recognize that, like everyone, they have vulnerabilities, fears, and struggles, fostering a sense of connection.
- **Read Empathy Literature:**
- Read literature or attend workshops on empathy. Gain insights into the various facets of empathy, including cognitive empathy (understanding someone's perspective) and emotional empathy (feeling someone's emotions).

4. Journaling:
- Start a forgiveness journal. Write down your feelings, the events that led to the need for forgiveness, and your evolving thoughts on the process. This helps bring clarity and release emotions.

5. Gratitude Practice:
- Integrate a gratitude practice into your daily routine. Focus on aspects of your life and relationships that bring joy, fostering a positive mindset that supports the forgiveness journey.

6. Mindfulness Meditation:
- Incorporate mindfulness meditation, specifically focused on forgiveness. Use guided meditations that explore forgiveness as a process, allowing you to release negative emotions.

7. Therapeutic Support:
- Seek therapeutic support if needed. Professional counselors or therapists can provide guidance, creating a safe space to explore and navigate the complexities of forgiveness.

8. Visualization Techniques:
- **Create a Mental Sanctuary:**
- Develop a mental sanctuary in your visualization. Picture a serene and calming place where you can retreat during moments of stress or conflict, fostering a sense of inner peace.
- **Symbolic Representations:**
- Use symbolic representations in your visualization. Incorporate symbols that represent forgiveness, healing, and positive transformation, such as a blooming flower or a serene landscape.
- **Progressive Visualization:**
- Practice progressive visualization. Gradually visualize the steps leading to forgiveness, including understanding, empathy, and the eventual release of resentment. This step-by-step process enhances clarity and acceptance.
- **Dialogue Visualization:**
- Engage in dialogue visualization. Picture a constructive and empathetic conversation with the person involved. Visualize expressing your feelings, listening actively, and mutually understanding each other.
- **Positive Outcome Imagery:**
- Focus on positive outcome imagery. Envision the positive changes that forgiveness can bring to your life and the life of the person involved, creating a mental image of a brighter and more harmonious future.
- **Integration of Senses:**
- Integrate the senses in your visualization. Include sensory details such as sounds, scents, and textures to make the mental image more vivid and emotionally resonant.
- **Future Visualization:**
- Incorporate future visualization. Envision a future where forgiveness has taken place, and both parties have grown positively from the experience. This forward-looking perspective reinforces a sense of hope and transformation.
- **Visualize Emotional Release:**
- Visualize emotional release. Picture the release of negative emotions and burdens associated with the situation, allowing a sense of lightness and liberation to emerge.

9. Affirmations:
- Integrate forgiveness affirmations into your daily routine. Repeat positive statements that reinforce your commitment to forgiveness and compassion, fostering a mindset shift.

10. Release Rituals:
- Create symbolic release rituals. This could involve writing a letter to the person you're forgiving (without sending it) and then ceremoniously letting it go, symbolizing emotional release.

11. Compassionate Self-Talk:
- Practice compassionate self-talk. Replace self-critical thoughts with kind and understanding language, acknowledging your own humanity and the imperfections that come with it.

12. Educate Yourself:
- Educate yourself on the benefits of forgiveness. Understanding the positive impact forgiveness has on mental, emotional, and even physical well-being can provide motivation.

13. Group Support:
- Join support groups focused on forgiveness. Connecting with others who are on a similar journey can provide shared insights, encouragement, and a sense of community.

14. Forgiveness Letters:
- Write a forgiveness letter. Express your feelings, articulate what needs to be forgiven, and convey your decision to release resentment. This letter can be for yourself or shared if appropriate.

15. Loving-Kindness Meditation:
- Engage in loving-kindness meditation.

Extend wishes for happiness, well-being, and forgiveness to yourself, the person involved, and all beings, cultivating a compassionate mindset.

16. **Set Boundaries:**
   - Establish healthy boundaries. Forgiveness doesn't necessarily mean re-establishing the same relationship dynamics. Clearly define and communicate your boundaries moving forward.

17. **Practice Self-Forgiveness:**
   - Extend forgiveness to yourself. Acknowledge and release any self-blame or guilt you may be carrying, recognizing that everyone is capable of making mistakes.

18. **Mindful Communication:**
   - If appropriate, engage in mindful communication with the person involved. Use "I" statements, express your feelings without blame, and focus on understanding each other.

19. **Affectionate Communication:**
   - Introduce affectionate communication. Share positive and appreciative words with others, emphasizing qualities you admire and fostering a more positive relationship.

20. **Mindful Walking for Release:**
   - Practice mindful walking as a physical expression of release. With each step, consciously let go of negative emotions, visualizing them dissipating into the ground.

21. **Forgiveness Workshops:**
   - Attend forgiveness workshops or seminars. These can provide structured guidance, practical tools, and a supportive environment for exploring the forgiveness process.

22. **Engage in Acts of Kindness:**
   - Engage in acts of kindness for yourself and others. Acts of kindness create positive energy, contributing to a more compassionate and forgiving mindset.

23. **Forgiveness as a Daily Intention:**
   - Set forgiveness as a daily intention. Each morning, affirm your commitment to forgiveness, creating a positive mindset that influences your interactions throughout the day.

24. **Celebrate Progress:**
   - Celebrate milestones in your forgiveness journey.
   - Acknowledge the progress you've made, whether it's a shift in mindset, a release of negative emotions, or improved relationships.

25. **Cultivate Patience:**
   - **Mindful Presence:**
   - Practice mindful presence. Be fully present in each moment of the forgiveness journey, allowing yourself to experience and navigate emotions without rushing the process.
   - **Acknowledge Feelings:**
   - Acknowledge and accept your feelings. Cultivate patience by recognizing that emotions associated with forgiveness may arise unpredictably, and it's okay to give yourself the time to understand and process them.
   - **Non-Judgmental Awareness:**
   - Develop non-judgmental awareness. Cultivate patience by observing your thoughts and emotions without harsh judgment. Allow yourself the space to explore and understand the complexities of forgiveness.

Part Eleven:
Putting It All Together

Chapter 1

Creating Your
Stress-Free Living Plan

1. **Self-Assessment:**
   - Begin by conducting a self-assessment. Identify specific stressors in your life, both external and internal. Reflect on how these stressors impact your well-being.
2. **Clarify Priorities:**
   - **Reflect on Values:**
   - Take time to reflect on your core values. What principles and beliefs are most important to you? Understanding your values provides a foundation for setting meaningful priorities.
   - **Identify Key Life Areas:**
   - Identify key areas of your life, such as relationships, career, health, personal development, and leisure.
     Recognize the unique priorities within each area that contribute to your overall well-being.
   - **Define Long-Term Goals:**
   - Clarify your long-term goals. Consider where you want to be in various aspects of your life, both personally and professionally. Long-term goals provide direction and purpose.
   - **Assess Current Commitments:**
   - Evaluate your current commitments and responsibilities. Are they aligned with your priorities and values? If not, consider adjustments to realign your actions with your core values.
3. **Set Realistic Goals:**
   - Set realistic and achievable goals. Break down larger goals into smaller, manageable steps. This approach minimizes overwhelm and provides a clear roadmap for success.
4. **Time Management:**
   - Implement effective time management. Create a schedule that balances work, personal life, and leisure activities. Prioritize tasks based on importance and deadlines, allowing for a more organized and stress-free daily routine.
5. **Boundaries:**
   - Establish clear boundaries. Clearly define boundaries in relationships, work, and personal time. Communicate these boundaries assertively to ensure a healthy balance and prevent unnecessary stress.
6. **Mindfulness Practices:**
   - Integrate mindfulness practices into your daily routine. Incorporate techniques such as meditation, deep breathing, or mindful walking to stay present and reduce the impact of stressors.
7. **Healthy Lifestyle Choices:**
   - Make healthy lifestyle choices. Prioritize regular exercise, nutritious meals, and adequate sleep. A well-nourished body is better equipped to handle stress.
8. **Social Connections:**
   - Cultivate meaningful social connections. Foster relationships that provide support, understanding, and positivity. Social connections act as a buffer against stress.
9. **Regular Health Check-ups:**
   - Schedule regular health check-ups.
     Proactively address physical health concerns through routine medical check-ups, ensuring that potential stressors related to health are identified early.
10. **Financial Planning:**
    - Develop a sound financial plan.
      Financial stability contributes to a sense of security, minimizing stress related to uncertainties. Create a budget, save, and invest wisely.
11. **Hobbies and Recreation:**
    - **Explore New Hobbies:**

- Be open to exploring new hobbies. Trying different activities exposes you to new experiences and can lead to discovering passions you may not have considered.
  - **Mix Solo and Group Activities:**
- Balance solo hobbies with group activities.
  Solo hobbies provide personal space and reflection, while group activities offer social engagement and shared experiences.
  - **Create a Hobby Space:**
- Dedicate a specific space for your hobbies. Whether it's a crafting corner, a reading nook, or a workshop, having a designated area enhances the enjoyment and commitment to your chosen activities.

12. Learning and Growth:
- Embrace continuous learning. Cultivate a mindset of curiosity and growth.
  Learning new skills can be empowering and can provide a positive outlet for stress.

13. Stress-Reduction Techniques:
- Learn and practice stress-reduction techniques. Explore techniques such as progressive muscle relaxation, guided imagery, or aromatherapy to find what works best for you.

14. Technology Detox:
- Implement technology detox periods. Set designated times to disconnect from electronic devices, reducing the constant stream of information and potential stressors.

15. Delegate Responsibilities:
- Delegate responsibilities when possible. Avoid taking on more than you can handle. Delegating tasks promotes efficiency and prevents burnout.

16. Positive Affirmations:
- Incorporate positive affirmations into your daily routine. Use affirmations to reinforce positive beliefs, boost self-esteem, and counteract negative thought patterns.

17. Gratitude Practice:
- Cultivate a gratitude practice. Regularly express gratitude for the positive aspects of your life. Focusing on what you're grateful for can shift your perspective and reduce stress.

18. Resilience Building:
- Build resilience. Develop a mindset that views challenges as opportunities for growth. Resilience enables you to bounce back from stressors more effectively.

19. Work-Life Integration:
- Seek work-life integration. Strive for a harmonious balance between work and personal life, recognizing that both aspects contribute to your overall well-being.

20. Emotional Intelligence:
- Develop emotional intelligence. Enhance your ability to recognize and manage your emotions, fostering better relationships and reducing interpersonal stress.

21. Conflict Resolution Skills:
- Strengthen conflict resolution skills. Learn effective communication techniques to address conflicts proactively and prevent unnecessary stress.

22. Nature Connection:
- Connect with nature. Spend time outdoors and engage in activities that bring you closer to nature. Nature has proven stress-reducing benefits.

23. Mindful Eating:
- Practice mindful eating. Pay attention to what and how you eat. Mindful eating promotes a healthy relationship with food and can contribute to stress reduction.

24. Quality Sleep Routine:
- Establish a quality sleep routine. Prioritize sleep by creating a calming bedtime routine and ensuring a comfortable sleep environment.

25. Regular Review and Adjustment:
- Regularly review and adjust your stress-free living plan. Life is dynamic, and priorities may change. Periodically reassess your plan and make adjustments to ensure its effectiveness.

Daily Routines for Sustained Peace

1. **Morning Mindfulness:**
   - Begin your day with mindfulness practices. This could include meditation, deep breathing exercises, or simply taking a few moments to set positive intentions for the day.
2. **Gratitude Journaling:**
   - **Daily Gratitude Ritual:**
   - Turn gratitude journaling into a daily ritual. Set aside a specific time each day to reflect on and write down the things you're grateful for. Consistency enhances the positive impact of this practice.
   - **Varied Gratitude Focus:**
   - Expand the focus of your gratitude entries. Express gratitude not only for significant events but also for small, everyday pleasures, interactions, or moments that bring joy.
   - **Specificity in Entries:**
   - Be specific in your entries. Instead of general statements, delve into the details of what you appreciate.
   Specificity adds depth and helps you savor the richness of each gratitude item.
   - **Gratitude for Challenges:**
   - Include challenges and difficulties in your gratitude reflections. Consider what you've learned or gained from challenging experiences, fostering a mindset of growth and resilience.
   - **Expressing Gratitude to Others:**
   - Use your gratitude journal as a platform to express thanks to others. Write letters of gratitude to friends, family, or colleagues, even if you don't intend to send them. The act of expressing gratitude can deepen relationships.
   - **Visual Gratitude Board:**
   - Create a visual gratitude board alongside your written journal. Use images, quotes, or symbols that represent the things you're thankful for. This multisensory approach enhances the impact of your gratitude practice.
3. **Hydration Ritual:**
   - Establish a morning hydration ritual by starting your day with a glass of water.
   Proper hydration contributes to physical well-being, enhancing your overall sense of balance.
4. **Healthy Breakfast Routine:**
   - Prioritize a nutritious breakfast. A well-balanced meal in the morning provides sustained energy and supports cognitive function throughout the day.
5. **Mindful Commute:**
   - If you commute, transform it into a mindful experience. Listen to calming music, podcasts, or practice deep breathing during your journey to create a positive transition into your day.
6. **Task Prioritization:**
   - Organize tasks and prioritize them based on importance. Tackling high-priority tasks first provides a sense of accomplishment and reduces stress associated with looming deadlines.
7. **Midday Recharge:**
   - Incorporate a midday recharge break. This could involve a short walk, stretching exercises, or a moment of mindfulness to refresh your mind and boost productivity.
8. **Lunchtime Mindfulness:**
   - Practice mindful eating during lunch. Pay attention to the flavors and textures of your food, and take a break from work to fully savor your meal.
9. **Afternoon Focus Session:**
   - Schedule focused work sessions in the afternoon. Identify a block of time where you can immerse yourself in important tasks without interruptions.
10. **Mindful Breathing Breaks:**
    - Integrate short mindful breathing breaks throughout the day. Pause for a few minutes to focus on your breath, bringing your attention back to the present moment.

11. **Digital Detox Hours:**
    - **Create a Dedicated Space:**
    - Designate a specific physical space for your digital detox. This could be a cozy corner in your home or a favorite spot in nature where you intentionally disconnect from electronic devices.
    - **Mindful Transition Rituals:**
    - Develop mindful transition rituals before and after digital detox hours.
      Engage in activities that signal the beginning or end of the detox period, such as a brief meditation, stretching exercises, or a short walk.
    - **Set Clear Boundaries:**
    - Clearly communicate your digital detox schedule to friends, family, or colleagues. Establishing clear boundaries helps manage expectations and minimizes the likelihood of interruptions during these hours.
    - **Digital Detox Calendar Events:**
    - Use calendar events or reminders to schedule digital detox hours. Treat these periods as non-negotiable appointments with yourself, prioritizing mental well-being over digital engagement.
    - **Family or Household Participation:**
    - Encourage family members or housemates to participate in digital detox hours together. Shared experiences foster a supportive environment and reinforce the importance of balance in the digital age.
    - **Offline Hobbies and Activities:**
    - Plan offline hobbies or activities for your digital detox hours. Engaging in pursuits like reading a physical book, cooking, or practicing a craft provides a fulfilling break from screen-based activities.
12. **Reflective Evening Walk:**
    - Take a reflective walk in the evening. This can serve as a transition from work to personal time, allowing you to clear your mind and appreciate the surroundings.
13. **Evening Unplugging Ritual:**
    - Establish an evening unplugging ritual. Turn off electronic devices at least an hour before bedtime to promote relaxation and improve sleep quality.
14. **Dinner Time Connection:**
    - Prioritize connection during dinner. Whether you're eating alone or with others, use this time to engage in meaningful conversations or practice mindful eating.
15. **Nightly Wind-Down Routine:**
    - Create a wind-down routine before bedtime. This could involve activities like reading a book, practicing gentle stretches, or listening to calming music to signal to your body that it's time to relax.
16. **Reflection Journal:**
    - Dedicate a few minutes before bedtime to reflect on your day. Journaling about your experiences, challenges, and gratitudes helps process emotions and promotes a sense of closure.
17. **Sleep Hygiene Practices:**
    - Implement good sleep hygiene practices. Ensure your sleep environment is conducive to rest, and establish a consistent sleep schedule to optimize the quality of your sleep.
18. **Screen-Free Bedroom:**
    - Keep electronic devices out of the bedroom. Creating a screen-free zone promotes better sleep and prevents the temptation to engage in stimulating activities before bedtime.
19. **Reading Ritual:**
    - **Curate a Relaxing Reading Space:**
    - Designate a specific area in your home as a cozy reading nook. Personalize it with comfortable seating, soft lighting, and a selection of your favorite books to create an inviting space for relaxation.
    - **Select Diverse Reading Materials:**
    - Incorporate a variety of reading materials into your ritual. Include fiction, non-fiction, poetry, or genres that align with your interests. Diversifying your reading choices can cater to different moods and preferences.

- **Unplug from Screens:**
- Before starting your reading ritual, unplug from electronic devices, including e-readers and smartphones. Opt for physical books to minimize screen exposure and create a more tactile and immersive reading experience.
- **Set a Reading Time Limit:**
- Establish a time limit for your reading ritual, ensuring it aligns with your bedtime routine. Setting a specific duration helps prevent unintentional late-night reading, promoting a healthy sleep schedule.
- **Introduce Ritualistic Lighting:**
- Enhance the ambiance of your reading ritual with ritualistic lighting. Consider using soft, warm-toned lamps or candles to create a soothing atmosphere conducive to relaxation.
- **Incorporate Gentle Background Music:**
- Experiment with gentle background music or ambient sounds while reading. Choose instrumental or nature-themed tracks to add a subtle layer of tranquility to your reading environment.

20. **Mindfulness Meditation Before Sleep:**
    - Practice mindfulness meditation before sleep. This can involve guided meditation or simply focusing on your breath to quiet the mind and prepare for rest.
21. **Gratitude Reflection:**
    - End your day with gratitude reflection. Take a moment to express gratitude for the positive aspects of your day, fostering a sense of contentment.
22. **Visualization for Tomorrow:**
    - Visualize positive outcomes for the next day. This forward-looking practice can instill a sense of optimism and readiness for the challenges and opportunities ahead.
23. **Consistent Sleep Schedule:**
    - Maintain a consistent sleep schedule, even on weekends. This helps regulate your body's internal clock, promoting better sleep quality and overall well-being.
24. **Mindful Tech Use:**
    - Be mindful of technology use before bedtime. Minimize exposure to screens and stimulating content to support a peaceful transition into sleep.
25. **Reflection on Peaceful Moments:**
    - **Gratitude Walks:**
    - Incorporate gratitude walks into your routine. During these walks, reflect on the beauty of your surroundings, expressing gratitude for the simple pleasures of nature, such as sunlight, fresh air, and the changing seasons.
    - **Savoring Daily Rituals:**
    - Engage in mindful savoring of daily rituals. Whether it's enjoying a cup of morning coffee, preparing a meal, or taking a moment to stretch, intentionally savor the sensory details of these routines to cultivate a sense of peace.
    - **Create a Peaceful Journal:**
    - Maintain a dedicated journal for recording peaceful moments. Regularly jot down instances that brought tranquility, joy, or a sense of accomplishment. Reviewing this journal becomes a source of positive reflection.

Measuring Your Progress:
Tools and Techniques

1. **Personal Well-Being Assessment:**
   - Conduct regular assessments of your well-being using well-established tools and questionnaires designed to measure various aspects of mental, emotional, and physical health. This provides quantitative insights into your overall progress.

2. **Stress Tracking Apps:**
   - Utilize stress tracking apps that help monitor stress levels over time. These apps often use self-reported data and can provide visualizations or reports, allowing you to identify patterns and trends in your stress levels.

3. **Mood Journals:**
   - **Daily Reflections:**
   - Take a few minutes each day to reflect on your emotions. Write down specific events or situations that influenced your mood.

4. **Physical Activity Logs:**
   - Keep a log of your physical activities, including exercise routines, yoga sessions, or mindful walks.
     Monitoring your physical activity provides a tangible record of efforts to stay active and promotes a healthier lifestyle.

5. **Sleep Trackers:**
   - Use sleep tracking devices or apps to monitor the quality and duration of your sleep. Analyzing sleep patterns can offer insights into your overall well-being.

6. **Mindfulness Timer:**
   - Incorporate mindfulness timers during meditation or relaxation exercises. These timers can help you gradually increase the duration of your mindfulness practices, indicating your progress in cultivating mindfulness and reducing stress.

7. **Energy Level Logs:**
   - **Morning vs. Evening Energy:**
   - Differentiate between morning and evening energy levels. Identify when you feel most alert and energetic as well as when fatigue tends to set in.
   - **Peak Productivity Times:**
   - Use the energy level log to pinpoint your peak productivity times.
     Schedule high-priority tasks and critical activities during these periods to capitalize on heightened focus and efficiency.

8. **Reflection Journals:**
   - Maintain reflection journals focused on specific areas of your life, such as work, relationships, or personal development.
     Regularly review these journals to identify patterns, set goals, and measure progress over time.

9. **Gratitude Tracker:**
   - Implement a gratitude tracker where you record daily moments of gratitude. Over time, this provides a visual representation of the positive aspects in your life, fostering a grateful mindset and indicating progress in cultivating positivity.

10. **Goal Achievement Checklists:**
    - Develop checklists for short-term and long-term goals related to stress management and well-being. Regularly review and update these checklists as you achieve milestones, providing a tangible measure of progress.

11. **Screen Time Monitoring:**
    - Track your daily screen time using apps or built-in features on devices. Excessive screen time can contribute to stress, and monitoring it helps you regulate your digital exposure for a more balanced lifestyle.

12. **Social Connection Log:**
    - Maintain a log of your social interactions. Note the frequency and quality of your social connections.

      Reflecting on this log helps you gauge your engagement in meaningful relationships and adjust as needed.

13. **Mindfulness Progress Diaries:**
    - Keep diaries specific to your mindfulness or meditation practices. Document your experiences, insights, and any challenges faced during these sessions. Reviewing these diaries allows you to measure your progress in cultivating mindfulness.

14. **Meal Planning and Nutrition Logs:**
    - Create logs for meal planning and nutrition. Track your dietary choices and note how they align with your well-being goals. Adjust your diet based on these observations for improved physical health.

15. **Financial Wellness Check:**
    - Regularly assess your financial wellness.

      Track your spending, savings, and progress toward financial goals. A healthy financial state contributes to reduced stress, and monitoring it ensures you stay on track.

16. **Relaxation Technique Records:**
    - Document the effectiveness of various relaxation techniques you employ, such as deep breathing, progressive muscle relaxation, or guided imagery. Note which techniques work best for you and refine your approach accordingly.

17. **Work-Life Balance Scorecard:**
    - Develop a scorecard for assessing your work-life balance. Consider factors such as workload, time spent on personal activities, and overall satisfaction.

18. **Self-Care Calendar:**
    - Create a self-care calendar where you schedule regular self-care activities. Track adherence to this calendar as it becomes a visual representation of your commitment to self-nurturing practices.

19. **Journaling for Stress Reduction:**
    - Utilize stress reduction journals to record stressors, coping mechanisms, and reflections on stressful situations. Over time, this helps you identify effective strategies and measure your ability to navigate stress.

20. **Emotional Intelligence Assessments:**
    - Engage in emotional intelligence assessments to measure your ability to recognize, understand, and manage emotions.

      This can guide your efforts in enhancing emotional resilience and well-being.

21. **Environmental Well-Being Checklist:**
    - Develop a checklist to assess your environmental well-being, considering factors like the organization of your living and working spaces. A clutter-free and organized environment contributes to a sense of balance.

22. **Spiritual Growth Reflections:**
    - Document your spiritual journey and reflections. Note experiences, insights, or practices that contribute to your spiritual well-being.

23. **Regular Health Checkups:**
    - Schedule regular health checkups to monitor physical health indicators. This includes blood pressure, cholesterol levels, and other relevant metrics. Maintaining good physical health is integral to overall well-being.

24. **Creativity Logs:**
    - Keep a log of creative endeavors, whether it's art, writing, or any form of expression. Monitor your engagement in creative activities as they contribute to stress relief and overall life satisfaction.

25. **Learning and Growth Records:**
    - Maintain records of your ongoing learning and personal development. Note books read, courses taken, or skills acquired. This reflects your commitment to continuous growth and development.

Overcoming Setbacks
and Maintaining Gains

1. **Resilience Building:**
   - **Mindset Shift:**
   - Foster a resilient mindset by viewing setbacks as opportunities for growth. Embrace challenges as part of the journey, and focus on learning from setbacks rather than dwelling on them.
2. **Reflective Practices:**
   - **Stream-of-Consciousness Writing:**
   - **Unfiltered Expression:**
   Allow your thoughts to flow freely onto paper without worrying about structure or grammar. This stream-of-consciousness approach can reveal underlying emotions and thoughts.
   - **Gratitude Journaling:**
   - **Positive Focus:**
   Dedicate a section of your journal to gratitude. Regularly express gratitude for positive aspects of your life, fostering a more optimistic outlook even during challenging times.
   - **Goal Reflection:**
   - **Alignment Check:**
   - Reflect on your goals and aspirations. Evaluate whether setbacks have led to a misalignment with your initial objectives, and consider adjusting your goals based on newfound insights.
   - **Problem-Solving Journal:**
   - **Solution-Oriented Approach:**
   - Create a section for problem-solving. Use your journal to brainstorm potential solutions to the challenges you're facing, encouraging a proactive and constructive mindset.
   - **Emotional Inventory:**
   - **Emotional Awareness:**
   - Conduct emotional check-ins. Regularly assess and record your emotional state. This practice enhances emotional intelligence and provides insights into patterns that may influence your reactions to setbacks.
   - **Learning Reflection:**
   - **Identify Lessons:**
   - Dedicate space to identify lessons learned from setbacks. What skills have you developed? How have you grown personally and professionally? This reflection reinforces a positive narrative.
   - **Future Visualization:**
   - **Visualizing Success:**
   - Visualize your future successes. Use your journal to describe, in detail, the positive outcomes you envision. Visualization can inspire motivation and help overcome the impact of setbacks.
3. **Adaptive Goal Setting:**
   - **Flexible Goals:**
   Adopt flexible goal-setting. Instead of rigid objectives, set goals that allow for adjustments in response to unforeseen circumstances. This flexibility promotes adaptability in the face of setbacks.
4. **Mindfulness and Acceptance:**
   - **Present-Moment Awareness:**
   Embrace mindfulness to stay present in the moment. Accept the reality of setbacks without judgment, allowing you to respond with greater clarity and resilience.
5. **Strategic Planning:**
   - **Strategic Evaluation:**
   - When setbacks occur, strategically evaluate the situation. Identify the factors contributing to the setback and formulate a plan to address them, emphasizing constructive solutions.

6. Support Systems:
- **Utilize Networks:**
- Lean on your support systems during challenging times. Share your setbacks with trusted friends, family, or mentors who can provide guidance, encouragement, and valuable perspectives.

7. Self-Compassion Practices:
- **Kind Self-Talk:**
- Practice self-compassion through kind and supportive self-talk. Treat yourself with the same understanding and encouragement you would offer a friend facing a setback.

8. Progress Acknowledgment:
- **Celebrate Small Wins:**
- Acknowledge and celebrate small achievements, even in the midst of setbacks. Recognizing progress, no matter how minor, reinforces a positive mindset and motivation to move forward.

9. Learning Orientation:
- **Continuous Learning:**
- Approach setbacks with a learning orientation. Consider them as opportunities for acquiring new knowledge, skills, and insights that contribute to personal and professional development.

10. Emotional Regulation:
- **Mindful Breathing:**
- Practice mindful breathing and other techniques for emotional regulation. Managing emotions effectively enhances resilience, preventing setbacks from derailing overall well-being.

11. Healthy Coping Mechanisms:
- **Healthy Outlets:**
- Channel stress and frustration into healthy coping mechanisms such as physical activity, creative pursuits, or engaging in activities that bring joy. These outlets contribute to emotional balance.

12. Holistic Wellness Practices:
- **Wellness Integration:**
- Maintain a holistic approach to well-being. Ensure that physical, mental, and emotional aspects are considered in your overall wellness plan, reinforcing your ability to bounce back from setbacks.

13. Time Management Adjustments:
- **Realistic Scheduling:**
- Adjust time management strategies to ensure realistic scheduling and workload distribution. Setting achievable targets reduces the likelihood of burnout and setbacks.

14. Reevaluation of Priorities:
- **Prioritization Review:**
- Periodically reevaluate your priorities. Ensure that your goals align with your values, and be willing to adjust them based on changing circumstances to minimize unnecessary stress.

15. Mind-Body Practices:
- **Yoga and Meditation:**
- Incorporate mind-body practices like yoga and meditation.
- These techniques foster a sense of calm and balance, contributing to mental resilience in the face of setbacks.

16. Problem-Solving Skills:
- **Structured Approach:**
- Develop strong problem-solving skills. Approach setbacks with a structured problem-solving mindset, breaking down challenges into manageable steps for resolution.

17. Gratitude Practices:
- **Focus on Positives:**
- Cultivate gratitude practices. Directing your focus towards positive aspects, even in the face of setbacks, can shift your perspective and promote emotional well-being.

18. Professional Guidance:
- **Seek Counseling:**
- If setbacks significantly impact mental health, consider seeking professional guidance from counselors or therapists. Professional support can provide valuable insights and coping strategies.

19. Visualizations for Resilience:
- **Future Success Imagery:**
- Practice visualizations that depict future success.
  Imagining positive outcomes can enhance resilience and motivation, helping to overcome setbacks with a renewed sense of purpose.

20. Networking and Collaboration:
- **Collaborative Solutions:**
- Engage in networking and collaboration. Seeking input from others can bring fresh perspectives and collaborative solutions, strengthening your ability to overcome setbacks.

21. Cognitive Restructuring:
- **Positive Reframing:**
- Implement cognitive restructuring techniques. Challenge negative thought patterns by reframing setbacks as opportunities for redirection and growth.

22. Consistent Self-Care:
- **Routine Well-Being Practices:**
- Maintain consistent self-care routines. Regular exercise, adequate sleep, and healthy nutrition contribute to overall resilience and better equip you to handle setbacks.

23. Active Problem Exploration:
- **Root Cause Analysis:**
- Approach setbacks with a systematic inquiry. Break down the situation into its components and investigate each aspect methodically.
- **Identify Contributing Factors:**
- Scrutinize all contributing factors. Beyond surface-level issues, delve into the underlying elements that may have played a role in the setback.
- **Ask "Why" Multiple Times:**
- Employ the "5 Whys" technique. Ask "why" repeatedly to identify deeper causes. This iterative process uncovers layers of causation, moving beyond immediate triggers.
- **Analyze External Factors:**
- Consider external influences. Evaluate how external factors, such as the current socio-economic climate or industry trends, may have contributed to the setback.
- **Internal Assessment:**
- If applicable, assess internal organizational dynamics. Explore how factors like communication, team collaboration, or resource allocation may have impacted the situation.
- **Evaluate Decision-Making:**
- Analyze decision-making processes.
  Examine whether the decisions made were based on accurate information, clear communication, and a thorough understanding of potential consequences.

24. Learning from Setbacks:
- **Continuous Improvement:**
- Approach setbacks as learning opportunities. Embrace a mindset of continuous improvement, using setbacks as stepping stones toward personal and professional advancement.

25. Community Engagement:
- **Community Involvement:**
- Get involved in community activities. Connecting with others who share similar experiences provides a sense of belonging and shared resilience, making it easier to navigate setbacks.

Chapter 5

Your Journey Ahead: Continuing the Practice of Stress-Free Living

1. **Reflective Review:**
   - **Periodic Self-Assessment:**
   - Engage in periodic self-assessment. Reflect on your stress management practices, identifying what has been effective and areas that may require adjustment.
2. **Mindfulness Integration:**
   - **Daily Mindfulness Moments:**
   - Integrate mindfulness into daily life. Incorporate brief mindfulness moments into routine activities, fostering a continuous awareness of the present moment.
3. **Gratitude Cultivation:**
   - **Gratitude Journaling:**
   - **Daily Reflections:** Keep a gratitude journal for daily reflections. Take a few minutes each day to write down three things you are thankful for. This can include simple pleasures, meaningful experiences, or the support of loved ones.
   - **Gratitude Jar or Box:**
   - **Tangible Appreciation:** Create a gratitude jar or box. Write down moments of gratitude on small notes and place them in the jar. Periodically revisit these notes to relive positive experiences and reinforce a sense of gratitude.
   - **Expressing Gratitude to Others:**
   - **Verbal or Written Appreciation:** Practice expressing gratitude to others. Whether through a heartfelt thank-you note or a sincere conversation, conveying appreciation strengthens your connections and uplifts both you and the recipient.
   - **Gratitude Meditation:**
   - **Guided Meditation Sessions:** Explore guided gratitude meditation. Dedicate time to mindfulness practices focused on gratitude, allowing yourself to immerse in the positive emotions associated with appreciation.
   - **Gratitude Walks:**
   - **Mindful Nature Connection:** Incorporate gratitude into your outdoor activities. During walks or hikes, reflect on the beauty of nature and express gratitude for the sights, sounds, and sensations around you.
   - **Gratitude for Challenges:**
   - **Finding Growth in Adversity:** Cultivate gratitude even in challenging times. Acknowledge the lessons and growth that adversity brings, reframing difficulties as opportunities for personal development.
   - **Gratitude Rituals with Others:**
   - **Family or Group Practices:** Introduce gratitude rituals within your family or social groups. Sharing moments of gratitude during meals or gatherings creates a positive atmosphere and reinforces collective appreciation.
4. **Adaptive Goal Setting:**
   - **Flexible Goal Planning:**
   - Adopt adaptive goal-setting. Set realistic and flexible goals, allowing for adjustments based on changing circumstances while maintaining a sense of purpose.
5. **Holistic Wellness Check:**
   - **Comprehensive Well-Being:**
   - Conduct a holistic wellness check. Assess various dimensions of well-being, including physical, emotional, social, and spiritual aspects, ensuring a balanced approach to self-care.
6. **Mindful Breathing Practices:**
   - **Focused Breath Breaks:**
   - Schedule short breaks throughout the day for focused breathing. Pause and engage in mindful breathing exercises to reset your mental state and enhance concentration.

- **Mindful Breathing Apps:**
- Utilize mindfulness apps that offer guided breathing exercises. These apps can provide structured sessions for various durations, accommodating your schedule and preferences.
- **Desk Meditation:**
- Integrate mindful breathing into your work routine. Take a few minutes at your desk to engage in mindful breathing, fostering a calm and focused mindset amidst daily tasks.
- **Mindful Breathing Alarms:**
- Set reminders or alarms on your devices to prompt mindful breathing sessions. This ensures regular intervals of relaxation and stress reduction integrated into your daily routine.
- **Breath Awareness during Transitions:**
- Practice conscious breathing during transitions between activities.
  Whether moving from work to leisure or vice versa, use these moments to center yourself through mindful breath awareness.

7. Regular Physical Activity:
- **Consistent Exercise Routine:**
- Maintain a regular exercise routine. Physical activity contributes to both physical and mental well-being, serving as a powerful stress management tool.

8. Social Connection Nurturing:
- **Quality Social Interactions:**
- Nurture social connections. Prioritize quality over quantity in social interactions, fostering meaningful relationships that provide support and connection.

9. Personalized Relaxation Techniques:
- **Nature Connection:**
- Spend time in natural surroundings as part of your relaxation routine. Whether it's a walk in the park, gardening, or simply sitting by a window with a view, connecting with nature can be deeply calming.
- **Creative Expression:**
- Engage in creative activities that resonate with you, such as painting, writing, or playing a musical instrument. Expressing yourself creatively serves as a therapeutic outlet and contributes to relaxation.
- **Customized Breathing Exercises:**
- Tailor breathing exercises to your preferences. Experiment with different techniques like box breathing, diaphragmatic breathing, or alternate nostril breathing, and adopt the ones that resonate with you the most.

10. Adaptable Time Management:
- **Ongoing Time Audits:**
- Continue time audits. Periodically assess how you allocate your time, making adjustments to maintain a balance between work, leisure, and self-care.

11. Continuous Learning Mindset:
- **Lifelong Learning:**
- Embrace a continuous learning mindset. Stay curious and seek opportunities for personal and professional growth, fostering a sense of accomplishment and adaptability.

12. Regular Digital Detox:
- **Scheduled Device Breaks:**
- Continue digital detox practices. Designate specific hours or days for a break from digital devices to reduce information overload and promote mental well-being.

13. Healthy Sleep Habits:
- **Prioritize Restorative Sleep:**
- Maintain healthy sleep habits. Prioritize restorative sleep by ensuring a consistent sleep schedule, creating a conducive sleep environment, and practicing relaxation before bedtime.

14. Adaptable Coping Strategies:
- **Versatile Coping Toolkit:**
- Expand your coping toolkit. Develop a repertoire of coping strategies and techniques, allowing for adaptability in managing different stressors.

15. **Mindful Decision-Making:**
   - **Conscious Decision-Making:**
   - Practice mindful decision-making. Before making decisions, take a moment to consider the potential impact on your well-being and align choices with your values.
16. **Emotional Intelligence Cultivation:**
   - **Empathy and Self-Compassion:**
   - Cultivate emotional intelligence. Foster empathy for others and practice self-compassion, creating a foundation for understanding and managing emotions effectively.
17. **Continued Social Support:**
   - **Building and Maintaining Connections:**
   - Continue building and maintaining social support. Actively engage with friends, family, or support groups to strengthen your network.
18. **Celebration of Achievements:**
   - **Acknowledging Progress:**
   - Celebrate achievements, big or small. Acknowledge and reward yourself for progress made in your stress management journey, reinforcing positive habits.
19. **Leisure and Hobby Integration:**
   - **Diverse Leisure Pursuits:**
   - Integrate diverse leisure activities. Explore new hobbies or revisit existing ones, ensuring a well-rounded and fulfilling range of recreational pursuits.
20. **Continuous Communication Improvement:**
   - **Clear and Open Communication:**
   - Foster continuous improvement in communication. Strive for clear, open, and empathetic communication to minimize misunderstandings and conflicts.
21. **Laughter and Playful Moments:**
   - **Joyful Interludes:**
   - Infuse laughter and play into your routine. Schedule moments for lightheartedness, whether through playful activities, humor, or shared laughter with others.
22. **Progressive Stress Management Techniques:**
   - **Expanding Stress-Reduction Toolkit:**
   - Expand your stress management toolkit. Stay informed about new techniques and strategies, incorporating them into your routine for continued effectiveness.
23. **Mindful Coping with Unexpected Events:**
   - **Adaptive Coping Strategies:**
   - Develop adaptive coping strategies. Cultivate resilience by approaching unexpected events with mindfulness and flexible problem-solving.
24. **Long-Term and Short-Term Balance:**
   - **Strategic Balance:**
   - Maintain a balance between long-term strategies and short-term relief. Blend practices that contribute to sustained well-being with those offering immediate stress relief.